BOOKER T. WASHINGTON
James Neyland

MELROSE SQUARE PUBLISHING COMPANY
LOS ANGELES, CALIFORNIA

JAMES NEYLAND is the author of numerous books, including *The Carter Family Scrapbook, The Battlestar Galatica Scrapbook, Write a Better Resume and Get a Better Job,* and *Politics, Fatcats & Honey-Money Boys.* For a number of years he worked as an editor for book publishers in New York. During the early 1960s he was active in the civil rights movement in his native Texas.

*In loving memory of
Christopher James Riccella
(1965–1992)
editor and dear friend.*

Consulting Editors for Melrose Square
Raymond Friday Locke
Mitchell S. Burkhardt

Originally published by Melrose Square, Los Angeles.
©1992 by James Neyland.

All rights reserved under International and Pan-American Copyright Conventions. No part of this book may be reproduced in any form or by electronic or mechanical means including information storage and retrieval systems without permission in writing from the publisher, except by a reviewer who may quote brief passages in a review. Published in the United States by Melrose Square Publishing Company, an imprint of Holloway House Publishing Company, 8060 Melrose Avenue, Los Angeles, California 90046. ©1992 by James Neyland.

Cover Painting: Lam Triet
Cover Design: Bill Skurski

BOOKER T. WASHINGTON

MELROSE SQUARE BLACK AMERICAN SERIES

ELLA FITZGERALD
singer
NAT TURNER
slave revolt leader
PAUL ROBESON
singer and actor
JACKIE ROBINSON
baseball great
LOUIS ARMSTRONG
musician
SCOTT JOPLIN
composer
MATTHEW HENSON
explorer
MALCOLM X
militant black leader
CHESTER HIMES
author
SOJOURNER TRUTH
antislavery activist
BILLIE HOLIDAY
singer
RICHARD WRIGHT
writer
ALTHEA GIBSON
tennis champion
JAMES BALDWIN
author
JESSE OWENS
olympics star
MARCUS GARVEY
black nationalist leader
SIDNEY POITIER
actor
WILMA RUDOLPH
track star
MUHAMMAD ALI
boxing champion
FREDERICK DOUGLASS
patriot & activist
MARTIN LUTHER KING, JR.
civil rights leader

CONTENTS

1
Dinner at the White House   9

2
Child of Slavery   19

3
Freedom and a New Kind of Slavery   35

4
Education   55

5
Educator   73

6
Building a Dream   93

7
Spokesman and Political Leader   113

8
The Niagra Movement and the NAACP   141

9
Betrayed by Violence   161

10
Past His Time   175

Chapter One

Dinner at the White House

THE EXECUTIVE MANSION IN Washington, D.C., showed its age; it was in serious need of repair. A bit of paint would have helped it live up to the name it had been called for years, "the White House," a name it would soon be given officially. However, to the dignified, well-dressed black man who was received courteously at the front entrance, it was a magnificent structure, one he had never even dreamed of seeing as a child living in a one-room log cabin with a dirt floor. Now he was to be a guest in this house for dinner.

Booker T. Washington had visited the Ex-

Booker T. Washington, founder of Tuskegee Institute, was recognized as the spokesman for, and leader of the African-American community throughout much of his lifetime.

ecutive Mansion on other occasions to meet with the previous occupant, President William McKinley, to whom he had served as an unofficial adviser on racial matters. Washington had greatly admired McKinley, not only because he sought to help the advancement of blacks but because of his ability to handle any situation calmly and with an appearance of confidence.

Washington still mourned McKinley's untimely death, shot by an assassin. It was October 16, 1901, just over a month since the Vice President, Theodore Roosevelt, had assumed the office, and no one was yet sure what kind of president he would be. At forty-three, Roosevelt was the youngest president ever, two years younger than Booker T. Washington himself. Most people thought of him mainly as the hero of the recently concluded Spanish-American War, leading his Rough Riders in the charge up San Juan Hill.

The White House butler escorted Washington past the brightly colored ornate Tiffany glass screens into the main entrance hall and then into the Oval Room, where the President, his wife, and three of his children were waiting.

When Washington stepped inside the beautifully decorated room, the President energetically bounded over to welcome him. The effect was startling. Roosevelt was actually a rather small man, but managed to create a large appearance by robust actions. His voice was high-pitched, almost shrill.

Mrs. Roosevelt was youthful, and quite gracious and charming. She was dressed elegantly and carried herself with dignity. The three children who were at home—Ethel, Archie, and Quentin—made Washington smile; they reminded him somewhat of his own high-spirited children when they were younger.

Although his host and hostess did everything possible to make Washington comfortable, he did not feel fully at ease, perhaps because he sensed they were not entirely comfortable. The occasion was highly unusual: no black person had ever been invited to dine officially at the White House.

Washington had eaten lunch with President McKinley at the Chicago Peace Jubilee, but that had been different; they had dined in public, both there for an official function. This was a private family dinner, which implied a degree of intimacy that was frowned upon among blacks and whites in the United States, particularly in the South, where Washington came from.

When dinner was announced, the President

escorted Washington into the dining room, while Mrs. Roosevelt ushered the children into place. The elegantly set table glistened with the shine of fine china and silverware, set upon a linen tablecloth.

He was grateful that in the years since slavery he had learned good manners and the proper use of a knife and fork. When he paused to think about it, the changes he had experienced had been incredible.

The President and Mrs. Roosevelt talked to him about his work at the Tuskegee Institute and about his approach to advancing the well-being of African-Americans through cooperation between southern whites and blacks, the spirit of compromise he had proposed at the Atlanta Exposition in 1895. It was what some were calling a "separate but equal" approach to racial problems.

At the conclusion of dinner, Roosevelt asked Washington if he would consider continuing to serve as an adviser on racial matters for him as he had done for McKinley. Honored by the request, Washington accepted but emphasized that it should not be in an official capacity; he had no desire for personal political gain.

It had been a wonderful evening, but the good feeling was not to last.

It was the custom in Washington, D.C., for

President Theodore Roosevelt shocked Americans when he invited Booker T. Washington to dine at the White House in 1901. No black man had ever dined there before.

The White House as it appeared at the time Washington was invited to dine there with President Roosevelt and his family. While Washington had visited the previous occupant, McKinley,

at the White House and served as his unofficial advisor on racial matters, he was severely criticized (as was Roosevelt) by the media for having dinner with a white man.

the local newspapers to print the official White House social calendar, and the next day the city was shocked to see that Booker T. Washington had been the President's guest for dinner. When the news was spread across the country, whites were outraged, especially those in the South. They felt betrayed, both by the President and by Washington, who had claimed that he favored the social separation of blacks and whites, that all he sought for his race was to attain legal and economic equality.

The press attacked both men, but they concentrated more on Washington because, as a black man, he should have known better than to accept the President's invitation. During the furor, neither Roosevelt nor Washington were willing to comment on the matter, hoping silence would help to calm the situation.

Finally most people accepted the view put forward by the white newspaper at Tuskegee, that "it is hardly the part of fairness to judge a man by one act with which we may not agree rather than by his twenty years of wise living. It is perfectly well known in this community that for fifteen years Prof. Washington's business in securing the money to carry on his work has thrown him into contact with the Northern white man both in the South and the North in a way that does not often fall to the lot of the average colored man."

This time Booker T. Washington would be forgiven for his "mistake," but he had become a public figure, and his every word and action would be watched carefully and judged severely. It did not matter that he had not sought public recognition for himself; it had been thrust upon him because he had stepped forward and spoken out in the hope of helping to resolve the growing racial conflict in the United States, while he might have chosen to live out his life in obscurity like most blacks in the South.

Having become a public figure, he could not turn back; he would face public scrutiny for the rest of his life; and that scrutiny would inevitably bring him criticism.

─────── *Chapter Two* ───────

Child of Slavery

I N THE SPRING OF 1856, there were doubts that the great experiment of democracy in the United States could long survive. The nation was growing increasingly divided along sectional lines, not only north and south, but west as well. The issue was slavery—whether or not that institution would be allowed to expand to any of the western territories that were seeking statehood—and it was rising to a bloody confrontation in Kansas between pro and anti-slavery settlers.

In May, the country was shocked at the news that a man named John Brown, with four of

---

Slavery so divided the American people, both north and south, that by the 1850s, there were doubts that "the great experiment of democracy in the United States" could survive much longer.

his sons and three other men, had massacred five pro-slavery settlers at Pottawatomie Creek, Kansas, in retaliation for the death of an anti-slavery man at a riot in Lawrence a few days before.

Just over a month earlier, on April 5, on a small tobacco plantation in Franklin County, Virginia, near the crossroads town of Hale's Ford, a woman named Jane gave birth to a son, whom she named Booker. The plantation belonged to James and Elizabeth Burroughs, and so did Jane and Booker, for they were slaves.

Burroughs was not a wealthy planter; he had 207 acres of land, but only 107 of it was "improved" and therefore able to be cultivated. He was like most southern farmers and slaveowners—constantly struggling to survive in an economic system that permitted only a few to live more than comfortably. At the time Booker was born, James Burroughs was sixty-two years old, and his wife Elizabeth was fifty-four; they were well past dreaming of making a fortune from planting. They continued to grow tobacco as a cash crop, but also grew what they needed to feed themselves and their slaves.

Tobacco crops require constant care and attention because of their susceptibility to mildew and other plant diseases and to the ravages of various insects. Burroughs and his sons, with a few slaves (his own and those hired out from neighbors), worked the fields, but by the 1850s he was short-handed, even for the few acres he planted. He and Elizabeth had fourteen children, but several had married and moved away. At most, he owned only ten slaves at one time, three of them Jane's young children, and Jane was employed full time as cook. Of the remainder, one was Jane's half-sister Sophia and three others were Sophia's young children. Only two were adult males, one Jane's half-brother Monroe. The other was probably the son of Sophia, and he died in 1861 at the age of twenty-three.

James and Elizabeth were not especially kind slaveowners, but neither were they extremely cruel. However, the system of slavery itself was sufficiently cruel as to make life almost unbearable to those who were slaves. Because of the system, Jane was not permitted to marry and establish a family. In fact, her first two children—John Henry and Booker—were both fathered by white men who never acknowledged their sons.

There has been considerable speculation about the identity of Booker's father. If he knew who it was himself, he never revealed the name. The most likely candidates include the Burroughs sons, James Burroughs himself, and neighboring planters such as Josiah Ferguson, who lived across the road from Burroughs.

One clue may be the fact that Jane secretly gave Booker the last name "Taliaferro" when he was born but never revealed the fact until years afterward. The Taliaferros were a very prominent family in Virginia and North Carolina at the time, and some branches, including an itinerant Baptist preacher named Harden Taliaferro (pronounced "Toliver"), lived not far from Hale's Ford. Of course, Jane could have conferred the name to her son purely out of respect or admiration.

The claims for James Burroughs being Booker's father rest primarily upon the statements of relatives that he and his uncle Monroe were "full-blood relatives." Monroe was not only Jane's half-brother, he was also the mulatto son of James by Jane's mother.

Although he had a white father, Booker was nonetheless a slave, and he was treated as one. As a young child he had tasks to do. In his autobiography, *Up from Slavery,* he recalled some of these. "During the period that I spent in slavery I was not large enough to be of much service, still I was occupied most of the time

John Brown. Booker T. Washington was still a child when the abolitionist began his fight against slavery. The action caused many whites to distrust their slaves, including Booker's owner.

in cleaning the yards, carrying water to the men in the fields, or going to the mill, to which I used to take the corn, once a week, to be ground. The mill was about three miles from the plantation. This work I always dreaded. The heavy bag of corn would be thrown across the back of the horse, and the corn divided about evenly on each side; but in some way, almost without exception, on these trips, the corn would so shift as to become unbalanced and would fall off the horse, and often I would fall with it. As I was not strong enough to reload the corn upon the horse, I would have to wait, sometimes for many hours, till a chance passer-by came along who would help me out of my trouble."

When he was older, Booker was also brought to the Burroughs house at mealtimes to operate the fan mill, an apparatus of paper fans worked by a pulley and strings, whose purpose was not so much to keep the master's family cool as to drive flies away from the table. For a time he even had the job of taking one of the Burroughs daughters to school on horseback, carrying her books, and returning home with the horse.

Even though his master was not a wealthy man, these contacts with the white family made Booker aware of the extreme differences between owners and slaves. The Burroughs family usually ate very well, while their slaves often went from the table hungry. On one occasion young Booker witnessed two of the Burroughs daughters, probably Laura and Ellen, eating ginger-cakes with their guests outside. Booker later recalled: "At the time those cakes seemed to me to be absolutely the most tempting and desirable things that I had ever seen; and I then and there resolved that, if I ever got free, the height of my ambition would be reached if I could get to the point where I could secure and eat ginger-cakes in the way that I saw those ladies doing."

Hunger was indelibly a part of his childhood. When Booker was assigned the job of stacking sweet potatoes in the root cellar, he admitted to taking one or two occasionally to roast in the fireplace for himself. And on one occasion he recalled his mother awakening him and his brother and sister to eat a chicken that she appeared to have taken without permission.

Booker later recalled the way the slaves ate: "On the plantation in Virginia, and even later, meals were gotten by the children very much as dumb animals get theirs. It was a piece of bread here and a scrap of meat there. It was a cup of milk at one time and some potatoes at another. Sometimes a portion of our family would eat out of the skillet or pot, while some one else would eat from a tin plate held on the knees, and often using nothing but the hands with which to hold the food."

Another strong memory of his childhood in slavery was that of the cold winters. The home that Jane occupied with her children was a small log structure that served as the plantation kitchen. Its floor was the bare earth, and its windows had no glass panes but were merely openings that let in the cold as well as the light. Although there was a fireplace for warmth as well as cooking, there were also numerous gaps in the walls and the door that let in the cold winter wind. Young Booker and his brother John Henry slept on a pile of dirty rags on the earthen floor.

John Henry was four years older than Booker, and he was very protective of his little brother. The most unbearable part of slavery for young Booker was the wearing of a new flax shirt. The fabric from which these shirts were made is not to be confused with linen, which is very soft and smooth against the skin. The flax shirts made for the slaves, and which were the only garments worn by slave children, were made from the rough, coarse leftover material of the flax plant. Until they were "broken in" by wearing for awhile, they were unbearably painful on a child's tender skin. Booker later described the feeling as like "a hundred small pinpoints" touching his skin. As a kindness to his little brother, John Henry would wear Booker's new flax shirts until they were soft enough to be bearable. The love and loyalty acquired between the two in childhood never wavered throughout their lives.

When Booker was three years old, in 1859, his mother gave birth to a daughter, his half-sister Amanda. This third child of Jane's had an acknowledged father; his name was Washington, called "Wash," and he was a slave belonging to Josiah Ferguson, who lived across the road from the Burroughs plantation. After the birth of Amanda, Jane would marry Wash and attempt to establish a family atmosphere for her children. For Booker, this was to have both advantages and disadvantages.

It is not known precisely where or how the child who grew up to be Booker T. Washington acquired his sense of values and his strict work ethic that stressed personal and racial achievement, for early in his life there appears to have been no positive role model other than his mother and John Henry. There are some indications that the very deprivation of a positive male role model created in him a desire to make one of himself. He did comment later in life on the fact that having a family heritage to live up to was an incentive for whites, and that not having one made achievement more difficult for blacks and failure easier to accept. He was determined to succeed in life at least partly because he wanted his children and grandchildren to have someone to look up to and to emulate.

Booker appears to have been influenced to some extent by members of the Burroughs family, the younger sons and daughters of James and Elizabeth, if not by his owners themselves. He was especially close to the twelfth child, Laura, who was fourteen years older than he, and to the fourteenth, Ellen, who was ten years older. Throughout their lives, he and "Aunt Laura" continued to correspond.

There is also the fact that Booker was at a most impressionable age when the Civil War began, and the battles came relatively close to the Burroughs plantation. Between the ages of five and nine, he overheard many conversations about the reasons for the war, both from the Burroughs slaves and the Burroughs family. At night, at home in the slave quarters, he heard his relatives talking about the injustice of slavery and the blessings of freedom.

As a child Booker T. Washington lived in a cabin similar to the one pictured above, and worked "cleaning yards, carrying water to the men in the fields and corn to the mill to be ground."

During the day, when he was working at the "big house," sweeping the yard or fanning flies at the dinner table, he saw that his owner's family suffered also, not only from the terrible war but from the institution of slavery. He perceived that they too were human beings who had inherited a system that now had to change.

On July 24, 1861, three days after the Battle of Manassas, better known as "Bull Run," James Burroughs died. He was sixty-seven years old; he left Elizabeth and his daughters to cope as well as they could with the plantation and the war, for his sons joined the Confederate Army as soon as they were able.

In November after the death of James, an inventory was taken of his estate, with a valuation placed on his possessions. Four-year-old Booker was valued at $400, while his eight-year-old brother John Henry was worth $550. Their mother Jane, who was now forty-one years old, was valued at only $250. For comparison, James' sorrel horse was valued at $140.

All of the Burroughs slaves remained on the plantation throughout the war, even though there were a few opportunities to escape safely under protection of the Union Army. They felt not only a responsibility toward their "owners," but a genuine affection and concern for them. Each night one of the slaves was selected to sleep at the "big house" to protect the Burroughs women, and Booker later stated that they would have laid down their lives to keep their mistresses safe if necessary. And when one of the Burroughs sons was killed during the war, the grief of the slaves was as deep as the family's.

This was not the case with the slaves of Josiah Ferguson, their neighbor across the road, because he was an especially cruel master, not only leasing out his slaves for backbreaking work in the salt furnaces, on railroad construction crews, and in the tobacco factories, but also beating them unmercifully for the slightest cause.

Booker's stepfather, Wash, was still owned by Ferguson, even though he had "married" Jane in 1859 when their daughter Amanda was born. They had managed to establish some kind of family life despite the fact that he was away on lease more often than he was home. In June of 1864, when the opportunity came for him to escape, he did so. It is not known whether or not he asked Jane to take the children and go with him. It seems likely that he did tell Jane of his plan to leave if given a chance, but considered his family safe and secure with the Burroughs women.

Wash's chance for freedom came when Union General David Hunter conducted a raid into Virginia that reached Lynchburg before retreating. Wash was working at a tobacco factory in Lynchburg at the time, and he, along with a great many other slaves, accompanied Hunter in his retreat north. Then Wash migrated to Kanawha County, West Virginia, where he easily found work at the Kanawha Salines because of his experience in the salt furnaces.

By this time the war was nearing an end. The tide had turned in favor of the Union. Not only were the Confederate troops suffering defeat in the fields, with high casualties, but the people at home, especially those in Virginia, the Carolinas, and Georgia, faced extreme food shortages because of the effective Union blockade of ports.

Booker's memories of his childhood hunger were probably from this period, because masters as well as slaves were threatened with starvation as the war was prolonged. He was only eight years old when Wash left and would be nine when the war ended. At the age when children most delight in play and the joy of discovery of the world around them, Booker knew only slavery and the suffering of war.

Later in life, he would ruefully comment that he had never been able to play games as a child, that he had not even known any. But he also acknowledged that he had not missed playing at the time because it had not occurred to him that there was any other way to spend his time than working.

It seems clear that Booker was not completely demoralized by the difficult circumstances of his childhood. He must have known laughter at least, and perhaps some degree of happiness, for the earliest known photographs reveal him to have a lively, almost impish quality in his expression, even though he is attempting to appear stern and dignified.

His appearance was rather striking, even as a child. He had alert but sensitive gray eyes, a medium brown complexion, and reddish hair. He looked at people when they spoke, meeting their gaze without hesitation, and he listened attentively. He walked with an erect posture and a determined gait, as if he knew where he was going and would get there despite all obstacles.

When freedom came, he would have the opportunity to try to do just that, but it would not be easy.

Chapter Three

Freedom and a New Kind of Slavery

FROM BIRTH TO THE grave, slaves longed for freedom, prayed for it, and dreamed of what they might do if—or when—it should come to them. Freedom meant having the right to make one's own decisions, to do what one wanted, to go anywhere, to have a last name and to marry and establish a family, to earn one's way in life, and to own property.

Yet when it did come, it was so abrupt and sudden that few slaves were prepared for freedom. They were faced with so many different decisions all at once that most were confused, and some were even frightened. The im-

Although President Abraham Lincoln had issued his Emancipation Proclamation much earlier, real emancipation did not come until the slaves were freed at the end of the Civil War.

mediate reaction of a great many slaves throughout the South was to set out on the road to go somewhere, anywhere, just because they could do so for the first time in their lives. But when they became hungry and had no means of buying food or found themselves in a strange place at nightfall with no place to stay, reality sank in. Some of these kept going, others returned to the only security they had known, to their owners, deciding to approach freedom gradually.

Emancipation did not come as soon as Lee surrendered at Appomattox Courthouse. In fact, it arrived in different states at different times, but all in 1865. The Virginia slaves were freed almost as soon as the war was over. On the Burroughs plantation, Booker recalled that the slaves knew some time in advance that freedom was coming, and that their nighttime singing in the slave quarters intensified, with much emotion put into lyrics containing the word "freedom."

The night before, word was sent to the slave quarters that an announcement was to be made at the "big house" the next morning. Everyone was sure they knew what the announcement was to be, and almost no one slept that night in anticipation. Early in the morning, Elizabeth Burroughs called the slaves to the house, and when they gathered the entire Burroughs family, including the sons who had returned from the war, were waiting on the veranda. The slaves stood in the yard facing the veranda, while a United States officer read the Emancipation Proclamation. After he finished, he told the slaves they were free to "go when and where they pleased."

With tears of joy running down her cheeks, Jane bent down to her children and kissed them; then she explained what had happened and what it meant for them. The slaves cheered joyfully, dancing about and hugging each other. But it did not last long. Booker later recalled: "The wild rejoicing on the part of the colored people lasted but for a brief period, for I noticed that by the time they returned to their cabins there was a change in their feelings. The great responsibility of being free, of having charge of themselves, of having to think and plan for themselves and their children, seemed to take possession of them. It was very much like suddenly turning a youth of ten or twelve years out into the world to provide for himself.

Most of the Burroughs slaves remained on the plantation with their former owners for a time, while they made the important decisions about their future. Elizabeth Burroughs and her children had to make similar decisions, for their lives were changing just as drastically as were the lives of their former slaves.

In August of 1865, Wash sent money for Jane to hire a wagon to bring their family to join him in West Virginia. After packing all their belongings into the wagon and saying goodbye to their relatives, Jane set out on the road with Booker, John Henry, and Amanda. It was the longest trip any of them had ever taken, more than 130 miles across the mountains, and they were several weeks on the road. Booker recalled that he and John Henry had to walk most of the way because there wasn't room for them in the wagon.

It was an exhausting and sometimes frightening ordeal for them. But, for Booker, it was mild compared to what he was to face when they reached their destination, the town of Malden in Kanawha County.

With freedom, Wash had taken on the last name of Ferguson in honor of his former owner, and he had also taken on some of the personality of Josiah as well, for he was as cruel and as dictatorial toward his stepsons as any slaveowner could be. Booker and John Henry were put to work immediately in the salt furnaces and their earnings turned over to Wash. Even worse were the circumstances

Booker's stepfather, Wash, took advantage of a raid by Union General David Hunter to obtain his freedom. He took himself to Kanawha County, West Virginia, where he found work.

in which they were forced to live.

Although the house that Wash provided for his family was not greatly different in size and construction from the cabin they had occupied on the Burroughs plantation, in one respect it was worse: it was crowded close to many other similar cabins occupied by the workers in the coal mines and salt furnaces of the area. Not only did this create highly unsanitary conditions, it also brought Jane and the children into contact with people, both black and white, of low moral character. According to Booker, "Drinking, gambling, quarrels, fights, and shockingly immoral practices were frequent."

At times Booker's workdays began at four in the morning, and often they would last until late in the afternoon. Booker did not complain about this, nor about his stepfather taking all his earnings, at least not until the opportunity arose for him to go to school to learn to read.

Ever since he had ridden to school with Laura and Ellen Burroughs to carry their books, Booker had longed to be able to read, to try to discover what great mysteries those books contained. It was one of the few goals he had created for himself in his young life, and he had great respect and admiration for anyone who had acquired the ability to create or decipher the mysterious markings that were supposed to represent letters or numbers.

He became quite excited at discovering he could recognize and even duplicate his first marking—the number "18." The workers in the salt furnaces packed barrels of salt, and each had a number. For Wash Ferguson and his stepsons, that number was 18, and eventually Booker was able to distinguish it from the other numbers.

This only added to his desire to know more. He pleaded with his mother to try to find him a book so that he could try to teach himself to read. Somehow Jane Ferguson managed to obtain a "blueback speller" for Booker, and he spent many hours leafing through it trying to make sense of it, without guidance from anyone who could recognize letters or words. (None of their neighbors in Malden could read or write.) After some time, he did manage to learn most of the alphabet, but could not put the letters together into words.

After he had been working at the salt furnaces for several months, Booker learned that a private school for blacks was being established by minister Lewis Rice in Malden, to be taught by a black man named William Davis who had recently come from Ohio. Booker desperately wanted to attend this school, but his stepfather refused to permit him; he needed the money that Booker was earning in the salt furnaces.

For a time Booker swallowed his disappointment and continued to work, even though he was able to see other boys and girls passing his workplace on their way to and from school every day, but he did not give up his determination. At every opportunity he mentioned his desire to his mother and stepfather. His mother sympathized with him and even encouraged him to keep up hope. It was probably she who arranged with Davis to give Booker lessons at night after his work was done.

He learned a great deal in those lessons, but they did not satisfy his yearning to attend the daytime classes with the other children. Finally, after several months of badgering from Booker, his stepfather agreed, but only on one condition: Booker would go to work at four in the morning and work until nine; then after school he would go back to work for another two hours. Booker accepted the stipulation happily.

Still there was a problem: classes started at the very time he was to be allowed to leave, and the schoolhouse was a considerable distance from the salt furnace. He often missed important parts of the lessons. His hours, like those of the other workers, were maintained by a large clock in the salt furnace office; the idea occurred to Booker that all he had to do to get to school on time was to set the clock ahead a half hour each morning. This worked until the supervisor discovered what was happening and put the clock inside a locked glass case.

It was because of school that Booker acquired his last name. From the time of his birth he had been called just "Booker." However, all of the other children had two names, which the teacher called for the attendance record; some had three. Booker decided himself to take the last name "Washington," only to learn after announcing this to his mother that she had given him the name "Taliaferro" at birth. Suddenly he had three names, which he kept— Booker Taliaferro Washington.

His brother John Henry took the name Washington as well, and his mother also conferred it onto James, a child the family adopted shortly after arriving in Malden when he was found abandoned in a stable. James was, at this time, about two or three years old.

Booker found it difficult attending day school and working a full day; when there were conflicts, work had to come first, so he frequently missed days or parts of days. Before

As a young boy, Booker found it difficult to attend school as he was employed at the salt furnaces with his stepfather, who insisted the family needed the money Booker and John Henry

earned. Throughout his childhood a thirst for knowledge caused him to find ways to attend as much school as possible and to seek out private lessons from local teachers.

long, with pressure from his stepfather, he had to give up day school entirely and return to try to obtain tutoring at night.

Davis, who was just ten years older than Booker, actually did not have much more than a rudimentary education himself. The classes he conducted included only reading and writing and the basics of geography and arithmetic, and Booker soon learned all Davis had to teach. As more schools for freedmen were established in the area, he tried other tutors, often having to walk many miles at night for his sessions, only to find that he knew more than most of them.

The frustration of these experiences did not deter him from his determination to obtain an education; if anything, it served to strengthen his resolve.

After Booker had been working at the salt furnace for a few years, one other thing occurred that made him even more determined to get the knowledge necessary to free himself of this new form of slavery he was living under. Wash Ferguson discovered his stepsons could earn more money for him by working in the local coal mines, which were operated primarily to supply fuel for the salt furnaces, and he obtained new jobs for them.

This would prove to be the most miserable

period of Booker's life.

He quickly grew to dread going to work. Working there was extremely dangerous. Accidents were common, because of mistakes made with the explosives or errors of judgment about how safe the tunnels and rooms were after blasts had cleared. Booker had to travel about a mile underground in total darkness to reach the rooms where the coal was being extracted. This was the most terrifying darkness imaginable, and a person did imagine the worst trying to travel about in it.

Booker did have a lamp to find his way about once he was down in the rooms, but frequently it would go out and he would be in pitch blackness until he could find someone to relight his lantern. Many times he would get lost and wander about in confusion, wondering if he would ever find his way out again.

There were two other factors that added to Booker's hatred of the coal mines. One was the coal dust that stuck to his skin and seemed impossible to get off no matter how much he washed and scrubbed. The other was an awareness he gained very quickly that the mines were very unhealthy; he perceived that many of those who worked there for prolonged periods were adversely affected, both mentally and physically. Those who were put to work as young children were especially prone to illness.

However, Booker gained one good thing from his work in the mines. It was there that he overheard a conversation between two miners about a college that had been established in Virginia especially for African-Americans. Instantly his curiosity was piqued. He later described: "In the darkness of the mine I noiselessly crept as close as I could to the two men who were talking."

One of the men mentioned the name: Hampton Normal and Agricultural Institute. As Booker listened, he learned more and grew increasingly excited. It sounded almost magical. It had never even occurred to him that such a place might exist, a place that taught all sorts of things, far beyond what was offered at the little schools around Malden, even the white schools.

Not only did Hampton teach trades and industry, but it also provided means by which poor students could work to pay for their board. "I resolved at once to go to that school," he later recalled, "although I had no idea where it was, or how many miles away, or how I was going to reach it; I remembered only that I was on fire constantly with one ambition, and that was to go to Hampton."

For a time that ambition seemed unattainable, nothing more than a dream or fantasy. Booker was stuck working in the coal mines, his money going to his stepfather to help pay the family's expenses. He could not be so irresponsible as to forget his family and simply set out on foot to try to find Hampton; even though the place sounded like Heaven, he would have to have at least a little money of his own.

First Booker had to get out of the coal mines. He knew that the longer he stayed there, the farther away his dreams would drift. It was several months later that his opportunity arrived. One day at work, he heard that General Lewis Ruffner, who owned the coal mines and the salt furnace, was looking for a servant to work at his house. Despite the fact that the Ruffner servants generally lasted only a few weeks at the job, Booker decided this was his chance.

The problem was that Mrs. Viola Ruffner, the general's wife, was extremely strict. She was a Yankee woman from Vermont, and no servant had ever been able to meet her high standards. Still, Booker had to try if he hoped to get out of the coal mines. So as not to miss work, he sent his mother to apply to Mrs. Ruffner for him.

Booker was hired, at a salary of five dollars a month. He was now about fourteen years old, soon to be fifteen. He was both elated at the prospect of working at the Ruffner home and terrified of facing the woman he had heard so many horrible stories about.

To Booker's surprise, Mrs. Ruffner wasn't really so bad once he understood what she expected of a servant. If something wasn't clean or tidy, or if something about the house noticeably needed repair, she expected an employee to have the initiative to take care of it without her having to point it out. When she called for a servant, she wanted him to appear promptly and to be honest and straightforward with her in all matters.

Booker found it was not difficult for him to meet these requirements. If there was litter on the lawn, he picked it up; if the front gate was off its hinges, he repaired it. He simply had to be alert to notice when something was out of order. This was to become a habit with him for the rest of his life. During the almost two years he worked in the Ruffner household, Mrs. Ruffner would prove to be a very strong influence in molding Booker's character.

She encouraged his desire for an education, and for a time allowed him an hour off each day to attend school, aware that his desire was

At the age of sixteen, Washington left home and traveled the five hundred miles to Hampton Institute in Virginia with virtually no money, determined to get an education.

genuine since he had the initiative to continue to attempt to find qualified tutors to help him in the evenings. Much of the time, however, this search was fruitless, and Booker found he could learn more by pursuing his studies entirely on his own.

In doing this he began to build what he called his "library," a small collection of books, which he kept in a bookshelf he constructed by knocking out one side of a dry-goods box and adding shelves to it. It did not matter to him what kind of books they were; any acquisition he could manage on his limited resources was a proud addition that he could learn something from.

The five dollars a month he earned working in the Ruffner household, like his earlier wages at the salt furnace and the coal mine, had to be turned over to his stepfather, although now he was permitted to keep a small amount for personal expenses, such as clothing or books for his library. Booker tried to put away as much of this as possible to pay his expenses to Hampton Institute, but after a year and a half he had managed to save only a few dollars.

Still, he was determined to go there, and he was not willing to wait much longer. By this time he had told his mother about his dream. She sympathized, but warned him it might be "a wild goose chase."

Finally Booker decided he had to go, with or without adequate funds. If he could just manage to get to Hampton, he was sure he could obtain some sort of work to survive; after all, he had heard that Hampton helped needy but worthy students earn their way.

As neighbors and friends in Malden began to learn about Booker's plan, many of them came forward offering whatever they could to help him on his way—some only a few pennies, others nothing more than a handkerchief or some food to take along. And John Henry offered to send him whatever he could spare from the part of his earnings he was permitted for personal expenses.

When Booker left he did not have even enough money to cover his fare by stagecoach and train and for lodging, but he set out anyway. His mother was fifty-two years old and in frail health; as he said goodbye to her, Booker feared it would be the last time he would see her. He loved her dearly, yet even that prospect would not deter him from his dream.

―――― *Chapter Four* ――――

Education

THE FIRST LEG OF Booker's journey to Hampton was taken by stagecoach, as there were no railroads in the Malden area. Booker was now sixteen years old, and the only long journey he had ever taken had been that with his mother, brother, and sister, from Hale's Ford to Malden, seven years before.

Booker faced his first obstacle when the stagecoach stopped for the night at a hotel in Virginia. The hotel was not very impressive, just an ordinary unpainted house. The other coach passengers went inside and arranged for accommodations. Booker waited shyly until

―――――――――――――――――――――――

A photograph of Booker T. Washington while he was attending Hampton. He worked constantly, after classes and during summer vacations to earn money for college—and graduated at the top of his class. Eventually a sponsor eased the way financially.

they were all taken care of and then approached the desk, even though he had no money to pay for a room or for food.

He was immediately turned away without even being asked whether or not he could pay. It was his first blatant experience with discrimination because of his color. It was September, and the weather was already cold in the Virginia mountains, but he had no choice other than to spend the night outside.

The rejection did have an effect upon Booker, but he did not dwell upon it because he was intent upon his objective of reaching Hampton. He would face other, similar experiences on his five-hundred-mile journey, but none of them would deter him.

Eventually he reached Richmond, Virginia, only eighty-two miles from his destination. This was the first large city he had ever seen, and it was a rather frightening experience for him. He was not only broke, but also exhausted and hungry, not having eaten for several days. Food vendors on the streets were selling fried chicken and half-moon fruit pies, and the smells from their stands added to Booker's agony. He later admitted that this was his moment of greatest weakness; he would willingly have given up his objective just for "a chicken leg or one of those pies."

That night, weak and dispirited, he managed to find a spot where he could sleep without being noticed—beneath a board sidewalk that was raised sufficiently for him to crawl under.

Walking about near the Richmond docks, he came upon a ship with a cargo of pig iron being unloaded. Approaching the captain, he offered to work in return for enough money to buy breakfast. The captain agreed, and he was so pleased with the job Booker did that he offered to hire him for the remainder of his time in port. Booker accepted eagerly; this would give him the funds he needed to proceed on to Hampton. By continuing to sleep under the sidewalk at night, he could keep most of his meager earnings for the last leg of the journey.

When he finally reached Hampton early in October of 1872, Booker had fifty cents remaining in his pocket, certainly not enough to pay for tuition at the Institute, much less for room and board. However, he had made it this far; he would not let such a small technicality deter him.

As soon as he arrived in Hampton, Booker found his way to the large, three-story brick building that was the Institute. He later recalled: "It seemed to me to be the largest and most beautiful building I had ever seen. The sight of it seemed to give me new life. I felt that a new kind of existence had now begun—that life would now have a new meaning."

He did not even consider what he looked like after such a long time on the road, sleeping on the ground, laboring for food. It had been days since he had bathed, and his clothes were dirty and ragged. Yet he set out directly to find the person who would assign him to classes at the school, naively thinking all he would have to do would be to ask and he would be admitted without question.

One of the great injustices of racial segregation is that it creates some degree of ignorance in the two or more races separated from each other. The more one is prevented from participating in the world around him, the greater his degree of naivete.

This naivete should never be used as a measure of native intelligence, as some white supremacists have done. African-Americans are no less and no more intelligent than people of any other race. If anyone who met Booker T. Washington his first day at Hampton had made a judgment about his intelligence, that judgment would have been that he was stupid or ignorant. With time, however, he proved himself to be a man of brilliant intelligence.

When Miss Mary Fletcher Mackie, Hampton's assistant principal in charge of the academic department, was faced with this young man who resembled a tramp more than he did a student, she did not dismiss him out of hand. Neither did she welcome him wholeheartedly. Instead she gave him a test.

After allowing Booker to wait in her office for several hours, while she accepted numerous other students, she finally approached him and commanded: "The adjoining recitation-room needs sweeping. Take the broom and sweep it."

Miss Mackie was a Yankee from New York, and her strict manner reminded Booker of Mrs. Ruffner's. Booker's common sense told him what she was doing, and he was determined to pass her test. He went into the recitation-room and began to clean it, not just sweeping but dusting as well, so that it would be spotless, just the way Mrs. Ruffner would have wanted it. He moved every piece of furniture, including desks and benches, so that no spot of dust would escape. And when he had finished with the room, he cleaned the closets.

When he had completed his task, Miss Mackie came in with her white handkerchief and tested everything for dust—not only the floor and furniture but the walls as well. Finally satisfied, she announced, "I guess you will do to enter this institution." To earn his board, Miss Mackie gave him a job as janitor.

Hampton Institute was still rather new at the time, having been established in 1868 by the American Missionary Association, an organization of northern antislavery missionary groups, specifically to educate black freedmen in the South after the Civil War. The Hampton catalog for 1874-75 described it as having been erected only a few miles from the site of the landing of the first slaves brought from Africa to America. In the spring before Booker's arrival there, the Virginia General Assembly had passed an act granting Hampton Institute one-third of the state's land-grant fund, some one-hundred-thousand acres.

Booker had much to learn, and it was not just from his classes in grammar, writing, composition, literature, mathematics, history, geography, and elocution. He also had to become acquainted with some of the basics of personal care and hygiene.

He recalled that it took him awhile to figure out why his bed was provided with two sheets. At first he slept on top of both, then underneath both, but finally, by observing the other students, realized that he was to sleep between them.

He quickly perceived the importance of personal care and became meticulous about hygiene. Although he owned but one pair of socks, he washed them by hand every night and hung them out to dry for the next day.

His job as janitor did not resolve all of Booker's financial problems. The ten dollars a month he earned barely took care of his room and board. Tuition cost seventy dollars, and his courses required books. Most of the time he was able to take care of this latter problem by borrowing books from more fortunate students. But tuition was another matter; he was already working as many hours a week as his classes permitted; there was no way he could raise that amount of money each year, even by working through the summers.

The solution to this problem came through Hampton principal General S.C. Armstrong, who also taught moral science and civil government. General Armstrong, who was to become one of Booker's closest and most loyal friends, admired the sixteen-year-old's determination and managed to persuade S. Griffits Morgan, of New Bedford, Massachusetts, to cover Booker's tuition for his entire course of study at Hampton.

Booker was one of Hampton's youngest students, some of whom were actually in their forties. He also became the favorite of several of his teachers, including Miss Mackie, who taught him mathematics.

Even so, there were numerous hardships for Booker, especially during his first year. He was embarrassed by the fact that he possessed only one suit of clothes, yet the students had to line up periodically for General Armstrong to inspect their grooming habits. Since Booker had to wear the same clothing for his job cleaning the buildings as he did for classes, he also had to spend some time every evening to polish his shoes and clean his clothes for the next day.

When his teachers learned of this they provided an extra suit from barrels of used clothing sent from northern charitable institutions, kept for such cases as Booker's.

It was also an embarrassment to him that he had no place to go during his summer vacation as the other students did. He could not afford to travel all the way home to West Virginia to visit his family, and it was rare for students to be permitted to remain at Hampton through the summer. He did not even have the funds to leave town to find work; in fact, he was in debt to the school sixteen dollars at the end of the term.

Eventually, after most of the students and teachers had left for the summer, Booker obtained a summer job not far from the Institute at a resort hotel belonging to Harrison Phoebus at Old Point Comfort, near Fortress Monroe. He spent his evenings reading and studying. His wages were only a little more than he needed for his board at the home of jeweler John L. Bentley, and he tried to save what he had left over to pay his debt to Hampton before entering his second year. However, by the end of the summer, he did not have anything near sixteen dollars.

Hampton's treasurer, J.F.B. Marshall, permitted Booker to delay repayment of his previous year's debt, and he was able to return to classes for his second year.

The following summer, in 1874, he went home to Malden to visit his family, aided by funds sent by his mother and brother and by a gift from one of his teachers. It was depressing to see the conditions his family and neighbors were living under. The salt furnaces weren't running, and the coal miners were on strike. Booker had hoped to be able to work while he was there, but no jobs were available because of the strike.

Concerned that he might not be able to return for another year if he did not find some way to earn money, Booker went to other communities nearby in search of some kind of job. One day he went to a town a considerable distance away. It was a long walk, and it proved fruitless. At nightfall, he began his return journey. As he drew near home, however, he was so exhausted he could walk no farther. When he came to an abandoned house, he decided to go inside to sleep for awhile.

Here John Henry found him about three o'clock in the morning. He had been out searching for his brother to tell him that their mother had died. The news was a great shock to Booker. She was only fifty-four years old. He had been aware for some time that Jane had not been in good health, but he had hoped that she would live long enough to see him complete his education. One of his great dreams had been to do well enough to provide her with comforts in her declining years.

For a time it appeared he would be unable to return to Hampton for his final year of study. His grief-stricken family was in chaos. Sixteen-year-old Amanda found it impossible to do all the housework and cooking that her mother had done. Wash, John Henry, and James were all out of work, and so far Booker had been unable to find a job.

However, as the summer progressed, Booker got work at a coal mine some distance from Malden, and Mrs. Ruffner paid him for doing odd jobs around her house when he had time available. He had misgivings about leaving his family in such dire straits, but he was determined to complete his education. He had managed to save enough money for his traveling expenses, when Miss Mackie wrote to him asking him to return to Hampton two weeks early to help her clean the buildings in preparation for the school year. The payment he would receive from this work would help him cover his debts to the Institute.

Booker had acquired both respect and affection for Miss Mackie, but now he grew to admire her even more. He had expected to work *for* her in cleaning the buildings; instead he found himself working *alongside* her. Not only was Miss Mackie educated and cultured, but she was from a very wealthy family; she did not have to work, especially not at scrubbing floors, washing windows, and changing beds, but she did so with energy and pleasure. She did not ask Booker to do anything that she did not also do herself.

Those two weeks taught him a lesson as important as any he had learned in his previous two years at Hampton—that physical labor was not something to try to avoid, that it was in fact something to seek out and achieve satisfaction from. This would be a lesson he would attempt to impart to others for the rest of his life. The purpose of education should not be for one to live a life of ease but to be able to work harder with a greater sense of achievement or accomplishment.

During his last year as a student at Hampton, Booker studied even more diligently than he had before, with his goal to be chosen one of the speakers at the commencement exercises. Not only would it be a distinct honor, but there was also the fact that he enjoyed public speaking. From his earliest time there he had participated in the debating societies and had even been instrumental in founding a new one.

He achieved his goal. At the graduation ceremonies on June 10, 1875, at the chapel of Virginia Hall, he was chosen to speak against the proposition for United States annexation of Cuba. From surviving newspaper accounts, he appears to have won the debate over his opponent, Robert Whiting. Young Washington's style was described as "terse and vigorous" by one listener and "terse, logical and lawyerlike" by another.

For his successful completion of three years of study at Hampton Institute, he was awarded a "Certificate of Achievement" that recommended him as "competent to teach a Graded school."

Christopher de Gasperi's drawing of a one room schoolhouse. In the 1870s such institutions gradually appeared throughout the South as more African-Americans realized the need for education.

This was what he chose to do. After spending a summer with other Hampton students working as a waiter at a hotel in Connecticut, Booker returned to Malden, West Virginia, to work in the school there, sharing the knowledge he had acquired with his friends and neighbors and their children. He later described this time as one of the happiest periods of his life. Not only was he able to help the townspeople who had helped him go to Hampton, he was also able to experience the joy of watching them change their lives in tangible ways, just as he had done.

He worked from eight in the morning until ten at night, teaching the young children during the day and giving night classes for the older, working children and the adults after the workday was over. On Sundays he taught Sunday school at Malden and also at another town nearby. He established a reading room and a debating society and tutored individual students who wanted to go on to Hampton.

One of the students he tutored was Miss Fanny Norton Smith, a childhood friend two years younger than he, who was the daughter of his family's Malden neighbors, Samuel and Celia Smith. Now in her late teens, Fanny had blossomed into an attractive young lady, and Booker was clearly smitten with her, but Fanny had ambitions for an education, and Booker valued her goals. If they talked of marriage, it is clear that they agreed to wait until Fanny could graduate from Hampton herself.

Of all the lessons Booker gave, it was those in personal hygiene that he found most gratifying. Lives were transformed by learning the importance of bathing, keeping clothes clean, and using a toothbrush. In *Up from Slavery*, he commented: "In all my teaching I have watched carefully the influence of the toothbrush, and I am convinced that there are few single agencies of civilization that are more far-reaching."

Yet all was not idyllic during the two years he spent teaching at Malden. The late 1870s saw the rise of the Ku Klux Klan, and this small community in the West Virginia mountains was not immune from it. This organization of night-riders was comprised principally of bitter whites who resented the political power of their black neighbors. Its objectives were to keep the now free African-Americans subjugated, to prevent them from advancing socially and economically, and ultimately to deny their newly acquired right to vote.

Most of the time their intimidation consisted only of anonymous threats, but when that did not work the Klan resorted to burning black churches and schools and finally to riots or murder.

Booker witnessed one terrifying riot in Malden, in which about a hundred blacks fought against roughly the same number of white "Ku Kluxers." A great many on both sides were injured. But the one case that saddened Booker most greatly was that of General Lewis Ruffner who stepped into the midst of the fight to try to protect the blacks. Seriously injured, General Ruffner later died of his wounds.

One thing that gave Booker great satisfaction in teaching at Malden was having the opportunity to prepare his brothers, John Henry and James, to attend Hampton Institute. His mother's great dream had been to instill a sense of family in her children, something slavery had denied her. Although Booker had not had the opportunity to reward her directly for her efforts, he was able to see that her wishes were fulfilled. For the rest of his life, he would hold the family tightly together and do all he could to help any member in need.

In the fall of 1878, Booker left Malden for further study, enrolling at Wayland Seminary in Washington, D.C. His ambition to go into the ministry was to be a brief one, however, for he left the seminary after only eight months, disappointed that Wayland, unlike Hampton, was not concerned with tangible human needs but with purely intellectual pursuits and with superficial appearances. In discussing the students here, Washington commented, "In a word, they did not appear to me to be beginning at the bottom, on a real, solid foundation, to the extent that they were at Hampton. They knew more about Latin and Greek when they left school, but they seemed to know less about life and its conditions as they would meet it at their homes."

Booker left Washington at the end of the school year to return to West Virginia. At the invitation of a group of white leaders of his state, he agreed to help campaign to have Charleston designated the capital of West Virginia because it was more centrally located than the previous capital of Wheeling.

Some were so impressed with his abilities that they tried to persuade him to seek a political career. While this was tempting, he decided he could do more for his race by concentrating his efforts in the field of education.

Chapter Five

Educator

EACH YEAR, HAMPTON WOULD invite a former student who had distinguished himself to return to the Institute to give a post-graduate address at the commencement exercises. In February of 1879, the principal, Samuel Chapman Armstrong, wrote to Booker Washington to invite him to give the address in May. For Booker, who was only twenty-three years old, this was a particular honor.

The subject of the speech he delivered on May 22 was "The Force that Wins." His actual words have not survived, but one account

Invited back to address the commencement exercise in May, 1879, only four years after his own graduation. This drawing from a 19th century magazine shows him practicing his speech.

of the time reported that "his address was an earnest appeal to his colored listeners to believe in patient, simple, dedicated labor in their efforts to help their race."

Gradually, a sense of mission had been growing and formulating in Washington's mind. Having acquired an education and become acquainted with the way the white man's world operated, he had obtained a special perspective: he understood why blacks remained in economic servitude despite freedom. It was the very reason so many of the former white masters had descended into poverty after the war. Knowledge was power, not just academic knowledge but an awareness of how to do things, whether it was to grow cotton or to build a house or shoe a horse.

For a time, during the Reconstruction period, the freedmen had been handed power without the knowledge needed to use it and keep it. Most blacks did not understand this. If they knew how to *do* things, they would also realize they could do something to lift themselves up economically. Money was also power, perhaps an even greater one than knowledge. When African-Americans had both money and education, they would not have to worry about discrimination or denial of rights.

Washington had learned this lesson; and it

became his mission to teach it to others of his race so that future generations would not have to suffer as he had.

Washington had not been back home in Malden for very long before General Armstrong contacted him again, this time to invite him to return to Hampton as a teacher in a new experimental program the Institute was developing—a course of study for native American Indians. He accepted the invitation eagerly, not only because it would give him the opportunity for post-graduate study but also because he would be able to try to put some of his strongly held beliefs into practice.

At the time it was generally assumed that Indians could not, or would not, be educated and "civilized" according to white men's concepts. Booker was taking a big chance by attempting to prove the contrary, and he was not fully confident that he could succeed. His job was made doubly difficult by the fact that the Indians considered the African-Americans inferior since they had accepted slavery, something no Indian would do. Indeed, many of the Indians had owned slaves before emancipation. There was also the fact that he would first have to teach them English before they could understand other lessons. This complicated matters further because the Indians were from a great many different tribes.

Booker began with Hampton's Indian program in the fall of 1879, not only teaching classes but later living in their dormitory, called "The Wigwam," with the new students, who numbered about seventy-five. This was a rather large enrollment, as the African-American students were only about twice that number.

To everyone's surprise most of the Indians learned English very quickly, and they responded eagerly and astutely to the industrial training. However, it took them awhile to comprehend the objective of reading and studying textbooks; at first they thought the purpose was to be able to carry large stacks of books from place to place. Although this fact is humorous, it does not imply that the Indians were stupid; rather, it points out that books were foreign to the Indian concepts of communication. Once they accepted the concept, they readily took to reading and study.

They quickly came to respect and eventually to love their teacher and dormitory supervisor. Booker later recalled: "I found that they were about like any other human beings; that they responded to kind treatment and resented ill-treatment. They were continually planning to do something that would add to

Dr. Robert Moton in the uniform he wore as Commandant of Cadets at Hampton Institute. He became administrator of the school and an inspiration to Washington.

my happiness and comfort."

For his second year of teaching at Hampton, Booker was given a new challenge. General Armstrong had decided to add a night school to the program, and he wanted Booker to take charge of it. Booker accepted enthusiastically; this was fully in line with the mission he had set for his life's work. He would be able to help educate those of his race whose economic circumstances prevented them from advancement, those who had to work full-time in order to survive.

It was a new concept. The students would work ten hours a day, the men in the school's sawmill and the women in the school's laundry, and they would attend classes for two hours in the evenings for a period of two years. Their earnings, beyond that needed for room and board, would be held in a fund to pay their expenses in attending day school after the two-year period was completed. Twelve students enrolled in the night school at the beginning, and within a few weeks the number had increased to twenty-five. It was so successful that it quickly became one of Hampton's most significant programs.

By his second year, Booker was earning thirty dollars a month in salary. What was left after payment for his room and board he contributed toward the expenses of his adopted brother James and his fiancee Fanny Norton Smith for their study at Hampton. John Henry was no longer at Hampton at this point, though Booker had helped to pay his way through the Institute a few years before.

Young Booker T. Washington, now twenty-five years old, was quickly establishing a reputation as an excellent and forceful educator. In May of 1881, near the end of his second year of teaching at Hampton, he was approached by General Armstrong with a question: would Booker be willing to undertake the management of a new normal school to be established for blacks in Alabama. Although Armstrong was expected to recommend a white person for the job, he considered Washington entirely capable of undertaking it.

Booker gave his consent, stating that he would be "willing to try." This was an enormous challenge, and he was probably both excited and terrified by the prospect. Up to this time, no African-American had ever taken on the responsibility of managing or supervising an institution of higher education in the South, and this job was not just to manage but to create one. If Booker should fail, he would not only disgrace himself but his race; if he should succeed, it would be proof of the abilities of

African-Americans.

The answer came in the form of a telegram delivered one Sunday evening during chapel services. The messenger delivered it to General Armstrong, who read it to the entire college after services were over. It stated: "Booker T. Washington will suit us. Send him at once."

On his way to the small town of Tuskegee in Macon County, Alabama, Booker stopped off in Malden, West Virginia, to visit with his family and friends for a few days, then proceeded to his destination—and as it turned out, to his destiny.

Upon arrival in Tuskegee early in June, his initial reaction was shock and dismay to learn that there was not even a building to house the new Tuskegee Institute. Although the Alabama legislature had provided an allocation of two-thousand dollars annually for the school, this was not to be used for buildings but only to pay salaries of teachers.

The bill to establish the Tuskegee Normal School, which had passed the Alabama legislature on February 10, 1881, provided for a board of three trustees, two of them white and one black. It was these men who had written to Armstrong at Hampton seeking someone to run the school. They were Lewis

Adams, a former slave, who now was co-owner with a white man of a hardware store; M.B. Swanson, one of Tuskegee's leading merchants; and Thomas B. Dyer, a dry goods merchant. On June 18, shortly after Washington's arrival at Tuskegee, Dyer died, and he was replaced by banker George W. Campbell, who became one of Washington's staunchest allies through the years.

Disappointed but not demoralized, Washington began to look for a suitable place to hold classes, aided by Lewis Adams. All they could come up with were the Butler's Chapel A.M.E. Zion Church and a shanty close by, both of which were in very dilapidated condition. In order to begin classes by July 4, he decided to use these temporarily, even though, when it rained, the roof leaked so badly that one of the students very kindly held an umbrella over Washington's head.

Adams and Washington did locate a prospective site for a permanent location, a hundred-acre plantation whose main house had been burned during the Civil War, but the owner, William Banks Bowen, was asking five-hundred dollars for it, with two-hundred of that in down payment, the rest to be mortgaged at eight percent. This seemed a fair price, though the trustees could not come up with

Booker T. Washington had never been to Tuskegee until after he accepted the challenge to head the new Institute. He was shocked on his arrival in Alabama. There was no campus.

Eventually one was established in the outbuildings (above) of a plantation whose main house had been burned during the Civil War. This drawing depicts the first campus.

the funds. Washington wrote to Hampton treasurer, James Fowle Baldwin Marshall, asking for his advice.

The two men corresponded on the matter, and Washington asked if Hampton Institute might be willing to loan the new school the needed two-hundred dollars. Marshall's response was that he had no authority to approve such an arrangement but that he could make a loan personally to Washington if it could be repaid by October. On July 9, Marshall sent his personal check, and Washington pledged his salary as collateral.

On the first day of school at the Methodist church, thirty students appeared. However, by the end of the month that number increased to fifty, and by the fall to seventy. The enthusiasm of the students and the Tuskegee community as a whole made up for the lack of school facilities. They were eager to learn and to help Washington in any way possible to get the Institute established.

Macon County was in what was referred to as the "Black Belt" of the South. Initially the label referred to the rich black soil of the region but with time came to apply to the area in which the black population outnumbered the white. In Macon County, the ratio was three blacks to one white, but in other areas of the Black Belt it was even greater. The town of Tuskegee itself had a total population of two-thousand, approximately half black and half white, and both races wanted to see the Institute succeed. Washington attributed this to the fact that the whites of Tuskegee were unusually well-educated themselves and desired harmony between the races. The cooperation was so successful that the town's hardware store was owned jointly by a black man (Tuskegee trustee Lewis Adams) and a white man.

Of course there were some whites who objected, fearing that educating blacks would result in their being unable to find workers for their farms or servants for their households, but those fears would eventually be put to rest.

Many of Tuskegee's first students were themselves teachers who had only the rudiments of education and had been employed at sharing what they knew with others but were now eager to learn more. About half were male and half were female, and many were well past youth. Almost all wanted to impress Booker and the other students with what knowledge they had managed to acquire.

Booker realized very quickly that one of the first lessons he would have to teach them was that the most important knowledge they could acquire was that which they could use in their everyday lives. While it was good to know Latin or Greek or French, these would not necessarily help them to earn their livings. At Tuskegee they would be required not only to study academic courses but also to acquire industrial skills.

Almost immediately, Washington realized that he had more work than he could handle alone. Teaching itself was a full-time job, yet he had to manage fund-raising, curriculum planning, and a building program, with very limited means. He wrote to several friends asking for assistance, among them J.F.B. Marshall at Hampton, who highly recommended Miss Olivia A. Davidson. However, Miss Davidson was in poor health and could not arrive at Tuskegee until the fall.

Meanwhile, Washington managed to hire two teachers to assist him for awhile, both graduates of Hampton—Miss Margaret E. Snodgrass and John W. Cardwell.

In September, Miss Davidson came to Tuskegee, fully recovered, and she proved to be a great asset in helping the Institute get started, assisting Booker with some of the managerial problems as well as teaching classes. She was a very attractive light-complexioned mulatto woman with a dignified, genteel demeanor and an intense fervor for work and for the advancement of educational opportunities for her race.

Miss Davidson had been born in Virginia in 1854, a slave of James C. Davidson, and she grew up in Albany, Ohio, where she attended the Albany Enterprise Academy. After completing her schooling there she and her brother Joseph went to Mississippi during Reconstruction to teach in a Freedmen's Bureau school. When Joseph was murdered by the Ku Klux Klan, she left Mississippi to teach in Memphis, Tennessee. In 1878 she went to Hampton Institute to pursue further education and graduated after only one year's study, disappointed that there was no more she could learn there. (Her tuition there was paid for by the wife of President Rutherford B. Hayes.)

Aided by funds provided by the aunt of one of her teachers at Hampton, Miss Davidson went on to Framingham State Normal School in Massachusetts, graduating after two years, in the spring of 1881, just before joining Washington at Tuskegee. Since she had obtained an even finer, more advanced education than Washington, she proved to be a great asset to the struggling school.

Booker had hoped to be able to move classes to the Bowen plantation by the fall, but that was impossible, although they had begun to clear some acreage for planting by the agricultural class in the hope that a cotton crop would aid the school financially. He did succeed in repaying Marshall's two-hundred-dollar loan on time as a result of donations, and by December 18, through various fund-raising efforts, he managed to pay off the remaining three-hundred dollars owed for "the old burnt place."

The only structures on the one-hundred acres acquired for Tuskegee were the cabin that had been used as the plantation dining room, the kitchen, a stable, and a hen-house. None of these structures were large enough to be used for assembling the entire student body, which grew to seventy and then eighty during this time. (By the end of the first year there would be 113 students.) It was necesary to continue use of the Methodist church for these colloquies.

However, the classroom needs were growing; out of necessity Washington and Miss Davidson decided to clean up the hen-house and the stable for use as recitation rooms. At first many of the students were unwilling to assist in the clean-up or in the labor of clearing the land for the school farm; but, following the example set by Miss Mackie at Hampton, Booker led the way, showing the students that there was nothing demeaning in hard work. In years afterward, it would be a source of some humor that many of the students had begun their classes in a hen-house and a stable.

By the end of the first school year, they were ready to lay the cornerstone for Tuskegee's first building, Porter Hall, named for Alfred Haynes Porter, a major contributor of funds. Washington decided it would be appropriate to hold the ceremonies as a part of the exercises commemorating that last day of the first session, March 30, 1882, the day that would have been commencement if the school had been operating long enough to graduate students.

The day was sunny and warm. After recitations by the students at the Methodist church, students, staff, and guests walked to the old Bowen farm, where the cornerstone was set in place, and then the county superintendent of schools, Waddy Thompson, spoke of the significance of the event. This was followed by a picnic dinner on the grounds of the future campus, in the shade of the old trees, after which the gathering returned to the church for singing and speeches by the students.

Just over two weeks later, on April 15, Booker T. Washington began a fund-raising tour of northern states, accompanied by Olivia Davidson. Washington went armed with letters of recommendation and the names of several wealthy philanthropists interested in the education of African-Americans.

For the most part, however, this first fundraising trip was disappointing. Booker and Miss Davidson were welcomed warmly, and the wealthy white northerners listened politely, but they either gave only small amounts or merely stated they would consider the request. A few gave letters of introduction to other potential donors. Most notable among these was the introduction by Moses Pierce, who had given two-hundred dollars toward paying off the land at Tuskegee, to John Fox Slater, a textile manufacturer who was to create the John F. Slater Fund for Negro Education.

Eventually these initial efforts would be rewarded by large donations from various quarters, but at the time it seemed hardly worth the tiring journey. When it was concluded in mid-July, Olivia Davidson was so exhausted that she went to Ohio to her family for a rest.

Booker returned to Malden to be married to his childhood sweetheart, Miss Fanny Norton Smith, who had finally graduated from Hampton Institute in the spring, aided financially by her fiance and teacher. Fanny had begun her studies at Hampton in 1877 but had been forced by financial reasons to stop for two years. During those two years, she taught school at Malden, paying off her debt and saving what she could for her return to Hampton.

The wedding ceremony of Booker T. Washington and Fanny N. Smith was conducted by Rev. I.C. Taylor, on August 2, 1882, at the home of Fanny's parents, Samuel and Celia Smith.

The couple did not take a honeymoon, but went to Tuskegee immediately after the ceremony in order to go to work preparing for the coming school year. They rented a house, and the other teachers boarded with them.

Chapter Six

Building A Dream

IT WAS BOOKER T. WASHINGTON'S belief that Tuskegee Normal School could make itself virtually self-sufficient through its industrial classes. If Tuskegee could become self-sufficient, so could African-Americans themselves. Fanny understood her husband's dream, and she shared it, for she had been there as Booker had developed it. It would take time for most of the other teachers hired to work at Tuskegee to comprehend what Washington was trying to do, for they had been trained to have pride in knowledge merely for the sake of knowledge.

The cornerstone of the first building of the new Tuskegee campus was in place by the end of the first school year. Porter Hall was named for a major contributor of funds.

Eventually, as Tuskegee grew, there would develop a jealousy between the academic and industrial departments; however, in the early years the new school was held together entirely by the powerful personality and boundless energy of its young leader. At the time of their marriage, Booker was twenty-six years old and Fanny was twenty-four; they made a very attractive couple. Fanny's father was part Shawnee Indian, and that heritage showed in her face, which was long and oval, with strong cheekbones and a straight nose. In her eyes, one could see a determination to endure any obstacle she might face.

During Tuskegee's second year, Booker's industrial trades education concept began to work because the students began to see results from their labor. The most visible sign of progress was the gradual rising of the three-story brick building that was to become Porter Hall.

Booker's belief was: "The individual who can do something that the world wants done will, in the end, make his way regardless of his race." And he proceeded to prove it. However, he faced considerable resistance at the beginning because of the myth that was being engendered among freedmen at the time that the purpose of education was to be able to avoid work. This belief was further encouraged by many of the early black ministers who were preaching that it was sinful to work.

During the first year, the physical labor asked of the students was primarily in the fields of agriculture and domestic science. Although there was some grumbling, most accepted it as a part of the price they had to pay for an education. During the second year, they were asked not only to labor in the construction of Porter Hall but also to work in the new brick factory. Others were employed in the carriage factory making the wagons and buggies needed by the school.

Letters poured in to Tuskegee from parents complaining about the way their children were being abused by being made to labor, and some even came in person to protest. A number of students left the school, having no desire to acquire useful skills. Those who remained to see the tangible results of their work learned the most important lesson Washington had to teach. They acquired a degree of pride in accomplishment that would serve them even more than the degrees they would get upon graduation.

It was a slow process, with the teachers often having to learn alongside the students, for there were numerous failures of the various industrial plants as they began to become established—brickmaking, sawmills, carriage manufacture, iron foundry, textile manufacture—before the most up-to-date techniques were mastered. In brickmaking alone, there were three expensive failures before they succeeded in producing usable bricks.

Yet by Thanksgiving Day of 1882, they were able to open Porter Hall officially, with services in the chapel presided over by Rev. Robert C. Bedford, white minister of the black Congregational church in Montgomery, Alabama. Those students who had built it were justly proud of their work. In the years that followed, if one of them caught a younger student attempting to carve his name into the brick, he would reprimand the culprit strongly.

It was not only the men's industrial program that faced problems that year. Fanny Washington had difficulties in getting her domestic services department underway. She wanted to start a boarding program for the students, but since she had not been present at the planning of Porter Hall no one had considered including a kitchen and dining room. Everyone had assumed that the students would continue to board at private homes in the community. However, Fanny considered this the ideal opportunity for teaching the women food preparation, cooking, and proper

Built almost entirely by student labor, Porter Hall was opened Thanksgiving Day of 1882. It was a beginning but Tuskegee still needed a kitchen, dining room and dorms for the students.

service.

Constructing a dining room and kitchen in the basement of Porter Hall proved to be the easy part, although it required digging out a great deal of earth around the foundation. Teaching her students to cook was the most difficult part for Fanny, who had the added stress of being pregnant during this time. Although the Tuskegee merchants willingly provided food supplies on credit, the school had virtually no equipment for cooking. Without a stove, it was necessary to prepare food over an open fire outside, with only a few donated pots, pans, and skillets.

The most difficult concept for the students was that meals should be served at set times, according to regular schedules. Most had come from poverty-stricken backgrounds similar to Booker's, where people ate whenever and however they could. During the first few weeks there was some kind of disaster with every meal. One morning there was no breakfast at all, and the young woman who had been assigned the job had even broken the rope attempting to draw water from the well. Booker overheard her complaining, "We can't even get water to drink at this school."

In spite of these difficulties, the whites of Tuskegee and in the northern states saw that the teachers and students were making a genuine, earnest effort, and they began to contribute, some with cash, others with supplies and materials. The blacks of Tuskegee and surrounding areas had been giving whatever they could from the very beginning, and they continued to do so, whether it was some change or a chicken or a few eggs.

Credit for the success was being given to Booker T. Washington and it was entirely deserved. The responsibility for making the Tuskegee concept work was entirely his, and it was a heavy burden for him to bear. He worked harder than anyone else, and he made sure that every debt was paid, and these factors contributed heavily to his growing reputation throughout the country. Combined with his strong character and his personal charisma, he seemed able to perform miracles.

On June 6, 1883, Fanny gave birth to a daughter, whom they named Portia Marshall Washington. The middle name was in honor of J.F.B. Marshall, who had believed in them and aided them in getting Tuskegee started. Her first name was given for the character in Shakespeare's *The Merchant of Venice*.

Before Portia was a year old, on May 4, 1884, her mother died, after a brief illness, at age twenty-six. The cause of Fanny

Washington's death is not known; it is believed to have been the result of injuries suffered in falling from a farm wagon. In late March, Booker was called home from his fund-raising trip north, which he had just begun, to return to Tuskegee to help care for Fanny. She was buried in what was to become the Tuskegee Institute Cemetery.

Booker was grief-stricken, and he now had the added burden of overseeing the care of a motherless child, but could not permit himself to neglect his duties to Tuskegee. Although he had to cancel his summer fund-raising efforts, he met all his other important obligations. He traveled to Hampton for the Alumni Association meeting on May 23, where he had the honor of presenting J.F.B. Marshall with an ebony, gold-headed cane in appreciation of his services, and appeared at Madison, Wisconsin, on July 16 for a speech before the National Education Association.

The Madison speech was to be the most important address made by Washington up to this point. The National Education Association was a prestigious organization, and the conference was attended by more than ten-thousand educators from all over the country, including white and black southerners. For the first time the conference was to feature concerns of African-American and Indian education, and a black educator—Booker T. Washington—was to address the group.

Racial tension surfaced at the outset, when black educators were at first denied their hotel rooms until the NEA officials threatened a lawsuit. Washington was given high praise for easing the tensions with his address, heard by four thousand of the educators attending. Those who had expected Washington to be extremely critical of white southerners were surprised. He concentrated on racial harmony, stating: "I repeat for emphasis that any work looking towards the permanent improvement of the Negro South must have for one of its aims the fitting of him to live friendly and peaceably with his white neighbors, both socially and politically. In spite of all talks of exodus, the Negro's home is permanently in the South: for coming to the bread-and-meat side of the question, the white man needs the Negro, and the Negro needs the white man."

Very subtly what Booker was proposing was a new era in race relations between blacks and whites. In the almost twenty years that had passed since the end of the Civil War, hostilities had increased to the point where the late 1870s and early 1880s were notorious for lynchings and violence provoked by the Ku

Ku Klux Klan riders. Washington, while teaching at Malden, West Virginia, was witness to a raid on the black community by "ku kluxers" who killed a white friend, General Lewis Ruffner.

Klux Klan, often with equally violent reactions from mobs of blacks. If this trend was to continue, Washington perceived that it would ultimately be detrimental to the advancement of his people, and he wanted to cool tempers at least long enough for African-Americans to obtain an economic foothold in society.

This speech proved beneficial to Washington personally as well as to Tuskegee. He was perceived as a reasonable and fair man, and contributions to the Institute increased rapidly, from whites not only in the North but in the South as well.

Although the tone of Washington's speech was conciliatory, he persistently refused to submit to racial abuse. Less than a year after the speech, in April of 1885, an incident occurred on the Cincinnati, Selma, and Mobile Railroad that prompted him to write a letter of protest to the Montgomery *Advertiser,* as well as one to railroad officials.

A group of teachers from Tuskegee were traveling on the railroad between Montgomery and Macon in a special first-class car arranged for the occasion. When they stopped at a small town at about the halfway point, some of their group stepped out onto the platform, since the train was to be there for twenty minutes. A group of lower-class whites noticed they had come from a first-class car and surrounded them with drawn guns threatening to kill them if they got back onto the car they had come from.

Before the train continued on its journey, railway officials forced the Tuskegee group to move to what was termed the "Jim Crow" car, which was little more than a boxcar, for the rest of the trip, even though the travelers had paid for first-class tickets.

At Macon, the group protested their treatment to the railroad superintendent. He apologized and provided them with a private car to their destination, Opelika, Alabama, but this did not make up for the insult.

Discrimination on railroads in the South would continue to be an issue for more than eighty years, even though many whites, including railroad management agreed that it was both unjust and economically foolish.

In May of 1885, Tuskegee held commencement services for its first graduating class. It was a very important event and a cause for celebration; the dream was being fulfilled, and that fact was clear to everyone. A second building had been completed, Alabama Hall, which served as a dormitory and dining hall. The student population had risen to two-hundred, and a reporter for the New York

Evening Post attending the ceremonies called Tuskegee "the most successful effort of the negro at self-education in this country."

The Institute now had a printing office, a carpenter shop, a laundry, a sewing school, in addition to the brickmaking plant and the forty-acre farm. The carpenters now not only made carriages, but also furniture of various kinds; the sewing room made all types of wearing apparel. Plans were in the works to add tinsmithing, blacksmithing, shoemaking, a sawmill, as well as fruit-canning and broom-making.

All of this meant even more work for Washington. Even though it seemed impossible, he increased his pace, traveling north for his usual summer fund-raising. Olivia Davidson accompanied him, but she soon had to return, suffering from exhaustion.

By October, Washington also collapsed and was hospitalized for ten days. Once recovered, he returned to work like a man obsessed, fully aware that much more had to be done before the success would be a lasting one.

On August 11, 1886, he and Olivia Davidson were married in Athens, Ohio, at the home of Olivia's sister Mary and her husband, Dr. Noah Elliott. Despite her frail health, the second Mrs. Washington took on the duties of housekeeping and looking after her stepdaughter Portia, while continuing to teach classes and to assist in fund-raising, working as hard as her husband, if not actually harder.

On May 29, 1887, Olivia gave birth to a son, named Baker Taliaferro Washington. His first name was given in honor of Eleanor Jameson Williams Baker, who had contributed large sums toward the establishment of Tuskegee. Later his name would be changed to Booker T. Washington, Jr. Olivia was thirty-three when she gave birth to Baker, two years older than her husband. Even though her health was frail, she does not appear to have suffered ill-effects from the birth.

This was not the case with their second child, Ernest Davidson Washington, called "Dave," who was born February 6, 1889. There were doubts whether mother and child would survive the birth, both having such a delicate constitution. To complicate matters, the Washingtons' house caught fire two days later, with a loss of almost all their belongings.

Olivia held onto life until May 9, when she died, just over a month short of her thirty-fifth birthday, leaving her husband with three young children to take care of, along with his many other burdens.

All of Tuskegee went into mourning. Booker

confessed that Olivia's loss was the deepest grief he had ever known, also commenting, "I never knew till her sickness how dearly she was loved and valued." She had been his staunchest ally almost from the beginning in creating his dream, working beside him for endless hours, a true partner long before they were married.

Yet Booker had to persevere despite all obstacles, even personal tragedy, for his goal was even more important than his own life or the lives of those he loved. He placed his three children in the care of the nurses at Tuskegee and later sent them to be cared for by a family in Massachusetts, where he saw them each summer during his fund-raising efforts.

The eight years of struggle to build Tuskegee had been hard ones. Washington was now thirty-three years old, but to those around him, he seemed older. Gone was the bouyant exuberant manner of the young idealist who had come to Alabama from Hampton, replaced by an appearance of strength and wisdom that could comprehend and overcome any hardship. Few people, other than his old teachers, called him "Booker" any more. He was "Mr. Washington" or "Dr. Washington" even to his closest friends.

It is likely that Washington himself was conscious of this transformation, but also aware that this public personna was necessary for the good of his cause. It could not have been easy, for even public figures have human feelings and failings. With Olivia gone, there was no one he could share his deepest thoughts with.

Even when he married again in 1892, his new wife generally chose to call him "Mr. Washington," finding it difficult to use his first name because of his great dignity. The third Mrs. Washington was Margaret James Murray, called "Maggie," who had come to Tuskegee in 1889 as a teacher and had been promoted to women's principal the following year. She was herself a rather impressive looking person, being considerably larger and sturdier than Washington's two previous wives. She was a very light mulatto with blue eyes, her father having been an Irish immigrant named James Murray. Her mother was Lucy Murray, a washerwoman at a railroad boarding house in Macon, Mississippi. Her birthdate is given officially as March 9, 1865, making her nine years younger than her husband.

Washington's children, especially Portia, had difficulty adjusting to their stepmother at first. To some extent this was due to Maggie's strict, rather haughty manner; in Portia's case, however, there appears also to have been a degree of jealousy, with the ten-year-old fearful of losing what little attention she received from her father. To ease family problems, Portia was sent away to boarding school.

As Booker T. Washington's reputation was spreading, he was increasingly being asked to appear to speak in various parts of the country. In 1888 alone there were three major speeches—to the Alabama State Teachers Association, to the Philosophian Lyceum of Lincoln University in Pennsylvania, and to the Unitarian Club of Boston. He was spending six months out of every year away from Tuskegee and for that reason it was necessary to have everything at the Institute so well organized that all of the details and many of the important matters could be handled by others without him. Tuskegee now had many excellent teachers and administrators by this time, all of them African-Americans; it became a matter of pride that Tuskegee achieved its success without direct involvement of whites. Perhaps the most important of the administrators during this time was treasurer Warren Logan, a Hampton graduate who had been hired in December of 1882.

As Washington's speaking engagements increased, he began to be looked upon more and more as a spokesman for his race. However, most still looked to the aging Frederick Douglass, now in his late seventies, as the leading voice for African-American concerns in the United States.

Douglass, born in Maryland about 1817 with the name Frederick Augustus Washington Bailey, was of a different mold from Booker T. Washington, and he held decidedly different views on race relations. He grew up under slavery well before the beginning of the Civil War and endured the worst of experiences associated with that institution. Escaping to Massachusetts in 1838, he joined the abolition movement in 1841, becoming a militant spokesman for black equality.

He was strongly opposed to any form of compromise, yet it appears that he valued what Washington was doing at Tuskegee, for he came there in 1892 to deliver the commencement address.

In 1895 Douglass died, leaving vacant his position as preeminent African-American spokesman. Almost immediately that position would be occupied by Booker T. Washington, who proclaimed a far different message from his predecessor's.

Chapter Seven

Spokesman and Political Leader

THE DECADES JUST BEFORE and just after the turn of the century were noted for a proliferation of world's fairs or international expositions, celebrating progress and industrial development. In 1885 there had been the New Orleans Exposition; in 1893, the Columbian Exposition in Chicago. In 1901, Buffalo, New York, would host the Pan-American Exposition; and in 1904, St. Louis would have the Louisiana Purchase Celebration.

In 1895, the big fair was the Atlanta Cotton States and International Exposition, held in Atlanta, Georgia. Booker T. Washington

---

When Frederick Douglass died in 1895, his position as African-American spokesman was almost immediatedly occupied by Booker T. Washington, who proclaimed a far different message.

was invited to give a brief speech at the opening ceremonies on September 18. Having spoken numerous times around the country, including an earlier speech in Atlanta in 1893 for the International Meeting of Christian Workers, it is doubtful if Washington had any idea in advance of the wide ramifications his words would have.

Of course he was quite aware of the historic nature of his appearance on the podium of dignitaries, and he fully realized the reason he had been invited. The civic and political leaders of Atlanta wanted to create a new image of their city and their state, to show that they were ready to shed the old idea of the South and to move forward in an enlightened way. This change of attitude was critical to getting the United States Congress to appropriate funds to help underwrite the exposition, and Washington had been one of three southern blacks asked by the Atlanta committee to appear before the congressional appropriations committee.

Racial harmony in the South was to be an emphasis at the exposition; for the first time at any world's fair, there was to be a "Negro Building," exhibiting the progress of African-Americans, with a focus on the success of Hampton and Tuskegee. The exposition committee trusted Washington not to offend southern whites in his remarks, and their trust proved not to be misplaced.

Everyone was aware of the historic nature of this event; never before had a black spokesman appeared before such a large gathering in the South. Southern newspapers began editorializing well in advance, almost as soon as it was announced that Washington would speak, not all of them favorably. Many white southerners were in attendance on September 18, some prepared to heckle or even riot. There were also many black southerners in attendance, proud that one of their race would be inaugurating the exposition.

Washington arrived in Atlanta by train the day before with Maggie and the children. Their train was met by a committee appointed by the Board of Directors of the exposition, which escorted them to their hotel. That night, Washington slept very little. In the morning he reviewed his speech very carefully, and then he knelt down and prayed.

The committee again came to the hotel to escort the Washingtons to the place where the parade would begin. It was a hot, sunny day in Atlanta, and the procession took three hours to reach the exposition grounds. Washington later commented: "When we reached the grounds, the heat, together with my nervous anxiety, made me feel as if I were about ready to collapse, and to feel that my address was not going to be a success."

The hall where he was to speak was packed, and there were thousands outside who had been unable to get in to hear him. He felt even more nervous than he usually did before making speeches. There were several on the program before him: the invocation, an ode of dedication, and speeches by the President of the Exposition and the President of the Woman's Board. Then former Georgia Governor Rufus Bullock introduced Washington. There was some applause, primarily from blacks in the audience.

Nervously, Booker rose to his feet and stepped to the center of the platform. Gazing out over the crowd, he was suddenly blinded by the afternoon sun glaring through the windows. He had to look away for a moment to adjust his eyes before beginning, standing erect and dignified before the crowd.

The reporter from the New York *World* perhaps said it best: "His voice rang out clear and true, and he paused impressively as he made each point. Within ten minutes the multitude was in an uproar of enthusiasm—

handkerchiefs were waved, canes were flourished, hats were tossed in the air. The fairest women of Georgia stood up and cheered. It was as if the orator had bewitched them."

The words he spoke were founded on reason and contained universal truths. Early in the speech he stated: "Our greatest danger is that in the great leap from slavery to freedom we may overlook the fact that the masses of us are to live by the productions of our hands, and fail to keep in mind that we shall prosper in proportion as we learn to dignify and glorify common labour and put brains and skill into the common occupations of life; shall prosper in proportion as we learn to draw the line between the superficial and the substantial, the ornamental gewgaws of life and the useful. No race can prosper till it learns that there is as much dignity in tilling a field as in writing a poem."

Near the end, he stated: "The wisest among my race understand that the agitation of questions of social equality is the extremest folly, and that progress in the enjoyment of all the privileges that will come to us must be the result of severe and constant struggle rather than of artificial forcing. No race that has anything to contribute to the markets of the world is long in any degree ostracized. It is important and right that all the privileges of the law be ours, but it is vastly more important that we be prepared for the exercises of these privileges."

However, it was in the middle of the speech, at its very heart that he spoke the words that became the most quoted afterward: "In all things that are purely social we can be as separate as the fingers, yet one as the hand in all things essential to mutual progress."

Those words, which became known as "the Atlanta Compromise," thrust Booker T. Washington, virtually overnight, into the position of a political and social leader, the most important spokesman for African-Americans of his time. It was a position he had so far endeavored to avoid, because he knew it would be detrimental to the more important mission, that of educating his people. He had wanted to set an example for his race; he had not wanted to use them as a source of power. Now he no longer had a choice.

Washington would be less successful in this role than he had been as an educator, for he was, from the outset, a man caught in the middle of widely divergent views. This new position also took precious time away from his work for Tuskegee, at the same time making

President Grover Cleveland was a good friend to Booker T. Washington and a stong supporter of Tuskegee, often making donations of cash when the school was in need.

his fund-raising activities somewhat easier because he and his views were well known.

On a later visit to the exposition, Washington had the opportunity to meet President Grover Cleveland and to escort him through the Negro Building. Washington commented: "As soon as I met Mr. Cleveland I became impressed with his simplicity, greatness, and rugged honesty. I have met him many times since then, both at public functions and at his private residence in Princeton, and the more I see of him the more I admire him. Mr. Cleveland has not only shown his friendship for me in many personal ways, but has always consented to do anything I have asked of him for our school. This he has done, whether it was to make a personal donation or to use his influence in securing the donations of others."

In June of 1896, Washington was given an honorary master's degree by Harvard University, the first African-American ever so honored. A few months later, early in 1897, he returned to Boston to speak at the dedication of the Robert Gould Shaw memorial, a statue sculpted by the noted Augustus Saint-Gaudens. Shaw had been the commander of the Fifty-fourth Massachusetts Regiment, comprised of black volunteers, which served the Union in the Civil War. Many of the men from that regiment attended the dedication. Again Washington gave a stirring address that was widely covered in the newspapers.

Washington's principal concern remained the growth and development of the Tuskegee Institute. So far the school had made great strides in every field except one—agriculture, one that Washington considered most important. The South remained a predominately agricultural region; therefore, it was essential that Tuskegee's agricultural department be the very best. In 1896, he found the man who would be able to fulfill that requirement, George Washington Carver, who had recently obtained his master's degree from Iowa State and was already achieving significant recognition.

He now believed he had Tuskegee so well organized that it could function effectively when he was away for extended periods. He had hired his brother John Henry as an administrator who could make decisions in his absence, and he had great trust and faith in Warren Logan. However, Washington had not expected Tuskegee to suffer the petty jealousies and animosities that are typical of white educational institutions, which now arose. Although Carver was not the cause of the problems that began to threaten the institution, the conflict initially focused on him because he was different—blacker, more educated, not from Hampton, and being paid a higher salary.

Although Washington did not have to handle all the problems himself, he was kept informed of them and was drawn into them more than he would have liked. In addition to this stress, there were family worries. He had tried to establish a stable home life for his children, but they seemed to want more attention than he was able to give. The hostility between Portia and Maggie had become so severe that Portia had been sent away to Framingham State Normal School in Massachusetts. Dave's delicate health was a constant worry, and Baker had turned to mischief-making to get attention.

Now that Washington had attained the level of a public figure, he became a target for attacks in the press. Since he was standing squarely in the middle, a spokesman for compromise, these attacks came from extremists on both sides—the southern white supremacists and the militant northern blacks. He was suffering stress in virtually every sphere of his life.

In his first two marriages, he had shared his

George Washington Carver was hired to head Tuskegee's agricultural department. He had just earned his master's degree and was resented by some of the older instructors.

heavy burdens with his wives, and it appears that he may have attributed their early deaths to this stress. Whatever the reason, he now kept most of his serious worries to himself, seeking escape from them in his relationship with Maggie.

In October of 1898, Washington was invited to give a series of speeches at the Chicago Peace Jubilee, celebrating the end of the Spanish-American War. One of these addresses would be before the largest crowd he had ever faced—an auditiorium packed with sixteen-thousand people. Here he met President William McKinley and members of his cabinet, and this would begin his close association with a series of presidents and high-ranking members of the Republican Party. He would become an unofficial presidential adviser on matters of concern to African-Americans, the leading figure in what was to become known as "the black cabinet."

The fact that Washington dined publicly with the President and white southern leaders while in Chicago became a matter of some comment in the southern press. However, the thing that drew fire from newspapers in the South was a reference he made to "the unjust discrimination that law and custom make against them (blacks) in their own country," in praising the heroism of black regiments at El Caney and Santiago in Cuba. The press complained that he was being two-faced, saying one thing in the North and another in the South. Washington defended himself, insisting he would not make any statement to northern liberals that he would not make at home.

During the next two months Washington traveled to Washington, D.C., twice to meet with President McKinley to persuade him to visit Tuskegee while he was attending the Peace Jubilee in Atlanta in December. It would, he believed, help to calm the racial strife that had been increasing in the South in recent months. The worst had been a race riot in Wilmington, Delaware, which had prompted whites throughout the South to urge disfranchisement laws—laws that would deny blacks the right to vote through literacy tests, poll taxes, and other means. McKinley agreed with Washington, coming to Tuskegee on December 16.

Of all the presidents Washington was associated with during his life, he was most impressed with McKinley, whose term was cut short by assassination. Not only did McKinley make numerous appointments of qualified blacks to governmental positions, but he was personally admirable. Washington said of him:

Washington, c. 1912. Booker T. Washington's close relationship with several presidents took him to the capitol often. In 1912, however, he strayed away. Former President Theodore Roosevelt

decided to run as an independent against the Republican nominee, President William Howard Taft, to whom B.T had also served as an advisor.

"I have observed that those who have accomplished the greatest results...are those who never grow excited or lose self-control, but are always calm, self-possessed, and polite. I think that President William McKinley is the best example of a man of this class that I have ever seen." It was an approach that Washington himself would strive to emulate.

By the spring of 1899, the various stresses Washington was having to endure had grown so severe he was close to losing his self-control. As he traveled to Boston for a fund-raising benefit for Tuskegee arranged by a group of Boston women, he was approaching total exhaustion. To appear with Washington at the Hollis Street Theater were two black writers who were achieving considerable renown—poet Paul Lawrence Dunbar, whose fourth volume of poetry was in the process of publication, and W.E.B. Du Bois, whose book *The Suppression of the Slave Trade* would prove to be only the beginning of a long and successful career. Maggie Washington was particularly pleased by this event, for Du Bois had been a classmate and good friend of hers during college.

At the social gathering after the event, Washington's Boston supporters commented on how tired he appeared and proposed that

President William McKinley, a friend to whom Booker T. Washington served as an unofficial advisor on racial matters. McKinley was shot and killed on October 16, 1901.

he take a rest by traveling to Europe. Washington protested that it was impossible for him to take time away from Tuskegee, only to be informed that everything had already been arranged. Not only had the group raised funds for others to do his work for several months, they had obtained the steamship tickets and planned his itinerary abroad. He was finally convinced by the argument that it would be detrimental to Tuskegee if he permitted his health to fail.

After eighteen years of intense and unceasing work, he was forced to take a vacation. He and Maggie set sail aboard the *Friesland* from New York City on May 10. Only after a couple of days at sea did Washington realize how tired he was. For the rest of their ten days at sea, he slept at least fifteen hours a day, and he continued to do so for a month after arriving in Europe. However, it was impossible for him to escape into anonymity, for his fame had already spread throughout the world. Everywhere he and Maggie went, they were invited to social functions and he was asked to speak publicly.

At first he accepted only a few of these invitations, cautious that too rigorous a schedule would defeat the purpose of the trip. Some were unavoidable and ultimately proved beneficial. At The Hague, they visited the peace conference. In Paris, they were guests with former President Benjamin Harrison at a banquet at the University Club. At a reception given by the American Ambassador to France, they met Supreme Court justices John Marshall Harlan and Melville Weston Fuller. Also they attended a showing of works by a black expatriate American painter, Henry O. Tanner, who had gained a considerable reputation in Paris, and they spent time with him.

But it was in England that the Washingtons would receive the greatest attention. Throughout the country, receptions and teas were given in their honor; and they received numerous invitations to weekends at country estates. At one reception given by the American Ambassador to England, Washington met Mark Twain for the first time; and on several visits to the House of Commons, he met with Sir Henry M. Stanley with whom he discussed conditions in Africa.

However, the greatest honor was their being received at Windsor Castle by Queen Victoria and being invited to have tea with her and another American guest, Susan B. Anthony. Washington later said of this occasion, "I was deeply impressed with the fact that one did not often get an opportunity to see, during the same hour, two women so remarkable in different ways as Susan B. Anthony and Queen Victoria."

After three months of viewing the world from a different perspective, the Washingtons set sail for home aboard the *St. Louis* from Southampton. There were honors waiting for him upon his return, the most touching being a tribute to him from the Mayor and City Council of Charleston, West Virginia, presided over by Governor George W. Atkinson.

On October 16, 1901, at the invitation of President Theodore Roosevelt, Washington would dine at the White House, the first African-American ever officially to do so as an honored guest. He and Roosevelt would both suffer much criticism from the white press in the South, Washington more so than Roosevelt, for this appeared to go against the promises made in the Atlanta Compromise.

With the arrival of the twentieth century would come a whirlwind of activity for Booker T Washington; at times the whirlwind would become a storm, with him at its center, but he held fast to his beliefs and his integrity. He was to endure the attacks he would receive, no matter what the source. His trip to Europe had taught him the value of relaxation as a balance to work, and he would now be able to

England's Queen Victoria greatly admired what Washington was doing at Tuskegee and invited him to lunch when he visited England, as did the King and Queen of Denmark.

let go from time to time.

In the beginning years of the new century, four books would be issued in his name though written by collaborators: *The Story of My Life and Work, Sowing and Reaping, Up from Slavery,* and *Character Building*. These works would not only increase his already high reputation but also spread his message. They also helped to attract funding to Tuskegee. George Eastman, the camera manufacturer, openly acknowledged that it was reading *Up from Slavery* that prompted him to donate to the Institute, initially only five-thousand dollars but then increasing it to ten-thousand annually.

In 1901, John D. Rockefeller, Jr., visited Tuskegee for the first time, as a guest of Robert C. Ogden on his private Pullman excursion. The following year, Rockefeller would provide the funds for building the three-story Rockefeller Hall on the Tuskegee campus. Also in 1902, after the completion of his twenty-thousand-dollar library on the campus, Andrew Carnegie was to give an endowment of ten-thousand a year.

Washington began to make an extra effort to try to resolve the problems with his children. Portia was now grown, and in 1900 graduated from Tuskegee after a year there.

For gaining the crucial financial support of Tuskegee Institute from such people as John D. Rockefeller, Washington was sharply criticized by northern blacks such as W. E. B. DuBois.

She studied at Tuskegee out of respect for her father but resented being forced to learn to sew. Insecure at eighteen, she had grown into something of an academic snob, perhaps influenced by members of her mother's family. After graduation, she went on to Wellesley College, but had difficulties there. Because of her color, she was not permitted to live on the college campus and had to stay in a boarding house. After a year at Wellesley, she left to attend Bradford Academy in Bradford, Massachusetts, from which she graduated in 1905.

Baker, now renamed "Booker, Jr.," was still high-spirited in his mid-teens. After studying in the training school at Tuskegee, he enrolled in the Wellesley School for Boys in 1902, though he had to leave after two years because of his rebellious antics. He had obtained a motorcycle, over his father's objections, and persisted in racing it at high speeds. As a result, Washington forced him to return to study at Tuskegee, where he graduated in 1905, going on afterward to study at Dummer Academy in Massachusetts.

Dave was the best liked of Washington's three children, though his health was always precarious. After attending the Tuskegee training school, he enrolled at Oberlin College in 1904, but had to drop out the following year because of an eye ailment that prevented him from using his eyes for six months. Concerned about the eye problem, Washington insisted on Dave staying at home and studying at Tuskegee, which he did. Later he would go on to a series of other schools, but continually had to drop out due to difficulties with his eyes.

Washington's sister Amanda Ferguson Johnston's daughter Clara graduated from Tuskegee in 1901 and returned to help her mother in her small restaurant business, which barely permitted the family to survive. (Amanda's son Albert had graduated from Tuskegee in 1893. Her two other sons would attend but not complete their education.)

In 1904, the Washingtons took in Maggie's nephew and niece, Thomas J. and Laura Murray, after the death of their parents. Thomas was almost grown, and he soon got a job at the Tuskegee Institute Savings Bank and moved out on his own. Laura, however, was very young, and the Washingtons adopted her to rear as their own child.

At times it seemed as if Washington would be completely overwhelmed by the numerous responsibilities thrust upon him in every facet of his life. In 1903, one of the largest fundraising benefits in Tuskegee's history was held at Madison Square Garden in New York, presided over by former President Grover Cleveland. That evening, Andrew Carnegie pledged $600,000, of which $150,000 was for the personal use of Washington and his family.

Washington was stunned and embarrassed by the gesture; he was well aware of how acceptance of such a sum personally might appear to others, and he felt compelled to refuse it. After some negotiating, a compromise was worked out in which that amount would be given to Tuskegee from which Washington would be paid his normal salary.

Almost immediately afterward there was to be a embarrassment of a totally different kind. Soon after the Atlanta Compromise speech, the northern black press, led by Monroe Trotter of the *Guardian* began to attack Washington, as well as to enlist supporters to help bring about Washington's downfall. Earlier in 1903, Trotter had made an unsuccessful attempt to overthrow Washington at the Louisville meeting of the Afro-American League, an organization of African-American leaders.

When Washington was invited to address the National Negro Business League in Boston, Trotter's home ground, the writer was determined to get attention. The meeting was scheduled for July 30, 1903, at the Columbus Avenue A.M.E. Church. Over two-thousand people packed into the hall to hear Washington. Among them were Trotter and a handful of his friends intent upon seeing that Washington would not be heard. They succeeded, first by heckling, then by starting a fight that developed into a riot that had to be quelled by the Boston police. Only after Trotter and three others were arrested was Washington permitted to speak.

When Washington supported the legal prosecution of Trotter and two of the others, W.E.B. Du Bois openly broke with his former friend to support Trotter, attacking Washington publicly.

That fall, Washington was again close to physical and emotional collapse. He left for Europe aboard the *Kaiser Wilhelm II,* as before sleeping most of the way across the Atlantic. While there, to avoid social and speaking engagements, he traveled incognito as "Homer P. Jones" and managed to get sufficient rest before returning in mid-October.

He was to need the rest, for he was about to enter even more troublesome times.

Chapter Eight

The Niagara Movement and the NAACP

DESPITE W.E.B. DU BOIS' public break with Booker T. Washington, the two men continued to cooperate to some extent. Until December 1904 they worked together to try to obtain repeal of the Tennessee Pullman Segregation Law, and they were associated in planning for the New York Conference to be held at Carnegie Hall, January 6-8, 1904, to bring southern whites, northern whites, and blacks together to discuss concerns of black voting rights in the South. Of course Monroe Trotter attacked the basis for the conference, claiming there was nothing to discuss as blacks

---

W.E.B. DuBois. Booker T. Washington continually made a distinction between racial problems in the South and those in the North. DuBois refused to see the difference and neither saw nor cared that Washington's friendship with wealthy whites was crucial to Tuskegee's growth and continual existence.

were guaranteed the right to vote by the Constitution.

Throughout the planning, Du Bois appeared to waver, as if torn between loyalties, aware of what Washington was attempting to accomplish in his quiet way but ultimately believing that Trotter's separatist approach was the only way to achieve success. Refreshed by his trip to Europe, Washington maintained hope that Du Bois' defection was only temporary, a manifestation of anger over the Boston Riot, even though Du Bois had attacked him viciously in his book, *The Souls of Black Folk*.

Washington may not have realized how divided black opinion was becoming; he had to some extent become insulated by his dedication to work and his associations with whites. However, he could not have helped but realize that African-Americans were going through the most severe hardships they had endured since the end of the Civil War, with ever increasing acts of violence against them, especially in the South. Yet he held to his belief that peace and reason were the only way to resolve black and white conflict. And he did have some evidence for his contention that whites would come around to accepting equal rights when they saw that blacks meant them no harm, that they had no intention of returning to the abuses of Reconstruction.

It may be that Washington perceived the importance of unity among blacks at this time, realizing that they could be most easily defeated if leadership became fragmented. He had reluctantly accepted the mantle of African-American leadership, but once given he would not readily let it go, especially to a self-appointed "leader" like Trotter.

Even though barred from the New York Conference, Monroe Trotter attacked it in the *Guardian*, doing everything he could to destroy it, and at the conference Du Bois and Clement Morgan endeavored to represent Trotter's contention that Washington did not reflect the majority black view, and that their race did not have to prove anything in order to have their rights guaranteed. However, the majority at the conference, both blacks and whites, did support Washington's approach.

The opposition was just beginning. Washington was to learn that northern and southern blacks were as different as northern and southern whites. However, it appears that, at least at first, he misjudged his opposition, thinking the dispute was little different from the differences between the academic and industrial departments at Tuskegee. On one level that was true, because it was a conflict between the elitist views of northern black intellectuals and the pragmatic approach of southern middle- and lower-class black workers who did not have much choice but to try to coexist with whites. What Washington failed to consider was the anger and resentment building among African-Americans against the rising tide of white oppression, not just the lynchings but also the new disfranchisement laws.

Washington appeared to be failing in the higher political arena as well. Even though he was an acknowledged but unofficial adviser to President Theodore Roosevelt, his words seemed to fall on deaf ears. The crafty hero of San Juan Hill gave lip-service to black advancement in government, but he perceived the political trend and, in actual practice, he cut back the number of black political appointments of his predecessor, William McKinley, despite Washington's appeals.

Reluctant to participate visibly and directly in politics, Washington did not attend the 1904 Republican convention in Chicago, but sent his assistant, Emmett Scott, to represent him in seeing that black southern delegates were accepted and in getting the "Negro planks" voicing opposition to black disfranchisement and lynchings onto the Republican platform. Here too he was ineffective. Still Washington supported Roosevelt in the election and continued to advise him on African-American matters after his reelection.

In the summer of 1905, W.E.B. Du Bois took matters into his own hands, calling black leaders from around the country to meet secretly with him in Buffalo, New York. After a racial incident at their hotel in Buffalo, the group moved to the Canadian side of Niagara Falls. Washington was pointedly not invited. They organized what was to become known as the Niagara Movement, with W.E.B. Du Bois as its leader, to actively protest racial injustice. The movement would grow slowly, but gradually African-Americans would look increasingly to Du Bois as their social and political leader rather than to Washington.

Meanwhile, Washington continued to pursue his approach of cooperation and personal diplomacy in the South. That year he began a series of speaking tours of southern states, starting with Arkansas, Oklahoma, and the Indian territories. He selected a few states each year, and he would spend a week to ten days in each, speaking at the major cities. It would take him six years to cover all the states.

Despite the fact that his image as a political leader was fading, he was met everywhere

In April, 1906, Tuskegee held its 25th anniversary celebration. Many prestigious people attended including Andrew Carnegie, seated at Booker T. Washington's right. At left is his third wife

Maggie. The strong willed Maggie had problems with Washington's children and especially the daughter, Portia, who was sent away to a boarding school to keep them apart.

with throngs of welcoming blacks and whites who applauded his message of accommodationism, of "separate but equal." However, it may have been the man they were applauding, not the message, for no one could deny what Booker T. Washington had achieved as an educator.

By this time Tuskegee was an acknowledged success, with every department functioning well, including the agricultural, even though there continued to be jealous attacks on George Washington Carver from other teachers. In April of 1906, Tuskegee held its twenty-fifth anniversary celebration, which came very close to coinciding with Washington's fiftieth birthday. A great many prestigious figures from all over the country attended, among them Andrew Carnegie.

The years of stress and overwork were clearly beginning to take their toll on Washington, not only physically but emotionally. He began to show signs of growing paranoia, which may or may not have been justified. Certainly he had received his share of crank letters and threats for years, and now he had become the object of espionage from Trotter and Du Bois, whose followers had secretly infiltrated Washington's inner circle. Other than his private secretary, Emmett Scott, Washington did not know whom to trust.

Washington has been heavily criticized for employing his own network of spies against Du Bois at this time, but he was only responding in kind to the treatment he had received. When he traveled, he also employed Pinkerton agents for protection, something he would never have considered only a few years before. Incredibly, he maintained a public image of strength and confidence, yet the isolation and uncertainty he was feeling showed in his eyes. It is evident in photographs taken of him during this period.

In 1906, racial strife in the United States would become particularly virulent and it would serve to weaken the view of accommodationism that Washington represented. The first eruption occurred in Brownsville, Texas, near the military installation of Fort Brown, on August 13. Before this night, there had been a few incidents of fights between blacks and whites in the town, blamed on the fact that black troops were stationed at the fort. It is not known precisely what happened that night, except that there was a shootout between a group of blacks and whites near one of the dance halls outside the fort. In it a white man was killed.

An armed mob of Brownsville citizens

gathered and marched on the fort, demanding that the black troops be punished. Officers at the fort promised an investigation of the matter; however, when questioned, all the black troops signed affidavits denying involvement in what had become known as "the Brownsville Riot." Assuming that the troops were lying to protect the guilty among them, the officers referred the matter to Secretary of War William Howard Taft, who in turn eventually referred it to President Roosevelt.

Meanwhile, on September 22, in Atlanta, an armed mob of whites marched into the black business district of the city, on Decatur Street, under the pretext that the liquor stores there were responsible for crimes committed in white areas by blacks. The rampage continued for five days, with the mob attacking any black person it could find. Many blacks fled the city. The Atlanta mayor and police appealed for reason, but the mob did not listen. When it was over, there were ten blacks and one white dead, as well as a number of stores, restaurants, and saloons in the area destroyed.

At the time the Atlanta Riot occurred, Washington was in New York, but he traveled to Atlanta afterward to do what he could to ease tensions. He also met with white and black leaders of Atlanta to make plans for working together in rebuilding the district.

On October 30, President Roosevelt called Washington to the White House to discuss the race riots, and especially to help him deal with the situation in Brownsville, which was still unresolved. The President's inclination was to dismiss the three companies of black troops wholesale since no one would admit knowing the cause of the riot. Washington tried to convince him that this was unjust. Both Brownsville and Atlanta were instances of white mob rule; surely if the situation were reversed, if a white soldier had shot a black citizen of Brownsville, the President would not dismiss all the white troops.

However, it was clear that Roosevelt's mind had been made up before calling Washington to the White House; he was seeing his "black adviser" merely as a formality. He proceeded to dismiss the entire black companies without trial, except for their white officers. If W.E.B. Du Bois needed proof that Booker T. Washington's approach of accommodationism did not work, he now had it.

However, Washington continued to believe in peaceful solutions to problems, pleading for the Christian response of "turning the other cheek." On Thanksgiving Day, he was back in Atlanta for the official formation of the Civic

League, organized by Charles T. Hopkins, a white attorney who had led the way in raising funds to aid the riot victims.

Washington also continued to try to convince President Roosevelt and Secretary of War William Howard Taft to do more than give lip-service to black advancement, to do something tangible to appease black voters by enlisting new black troops to replace those dismissed and by appointing black military officers in command of black troops. But neither heeded his requests.

Roosevelt's betrayal of Washington was most blatant in his message to Congress in December of 1906. Despite Washington's request to the President to tone down his speech, Roosevelt took the stance of the most racist white southerners in his attack on black criminality, justifying the lynching of blacks as a lesser crime than that of black men raping white women, which he claimed as the cause of lynchings.

The claims were outrageous, serving to foster southern white fears and to encourage the myth that blacks were inherently criminal. The speech promoted racial violence and set back understanding between whites and blacks for many years. It was also an embarrassment for Washington, the President's adviser on racial matters, because there was the implication that he agreed with what Roosevelt said, having read the speech in advance.

Meanwhile Washington's relationships with his children were improving as they were growing to adulthood, though there were invariably minor problems. During this time, Portia was in Berlin, where she was studying music. Because of the racial climate in the United States she was considering remaining in Europe even after her studies were over. However, her father persuaded her to return home, which she did. On October 31, 1907, she was married to Tuskegee graduate William Sidney Pitman, an architect now of Washington, D.C., in an elaborate ceremony on the Tuskegee campus.

That same year, Dave finally graduated from Tuskegee, and Booker Jr. left Phillips Exeter Academy to enroll in Fisk University in Nashville.

During 1907, Washington worked very hard to promote the "separate but equal" concept, not only through his speeches on his tour of southern states but also in speeches before important bodies such as the Conference for Education in the South. He helped raise funds for the formation of white Law and Order clubs, and met privately with liberal white southern leaders. The racial question during this time unfortunately became closely linked with the Prohibition movement. Many whites believed that black crime was encouraged by alcohol consumption, and the crime that most terrified whites was rape. This attitude was instrumental in the southern states banning or regulating alcohol sales and consumption. Washington spoke out in favor of Prohibition, and this fact came across as acknowledgment that alcohol was a problem for blacks and a cause of the rape of white women, which was not what he had intended to convey.

Washington's efforts intensified in 1908 and 1909, but so did those of his opposition, who endeavored to make him look like an "Uncle Tom." This was easy to do because Washington preferred to work quietly behind the scenes to change unjust laws, seeking no recognition for his efforts. One such case began in 1908, that of Alonzo Bailey, who had been tried and convicted under the peonage statute of the State of Alabama. Bailey had contracted to work as a farm laborer on salary, then had taken an advance against the salary, and had left employment before repaying the debt. Washington believed that such "involuntary peonage" laws were unjust, and for three years he pushed the Bailey case all the way up to the

Supreme Court, which in 1911 finally declared peonage laws unconstitutional.

Also in 1908, the African nation of Liberia was suffering severe financial problems, and it sent representatives to Booker T. Washington to enlist his aid in getting the U.S. government to intercede with their creditors, England, France, and Germany. Washington did as they asked, and the President sent a commission to investigate, then after receiving the report initiated a bill in Congress to establish a protectorate over the African nation until its financial problems were resolved.

That same year, Olivia E. Phelps Stokes established a scholarship fund at Tuskegee for the education of Liberian students and began to make plans for establishing the Booker T. Washington Industrial Institute in Liberia. Despite his willingness to aid African nations, however, Washington did not believe that any large-scale back-to-Africa movement could work. After generations in the New World, he perceived that African-Americans had become too Americanized to adjust to conditions and social conditions on their ancestral continent.

To some extent this view had been influenced by Tuskegee-sponsored projects in Africa, in which students voluntarily went to Africa to educate the natives, the first having been in Togo in 1900. Unprepared for the hardships they would face in Africa, many students died and others returned to the U.S. completely demoralized.

Washington continued to believe that African-American hopes for advancement were linked to the Republican Party, and 1908 was a presidential election year. Roosevelt's Secretary of War, William Howard Taft, had a clear edge over other candidates to be the Republican candidate for president. However, blacks could not help but recall Taft's unsavory involvement in the outcome of the Brownsville Riot. Again the convention was held in Chicago, and again Washington refused to participate directly.

Neither Washington nor Taft was able to find a prominent African-American to make the traditional black seconding speech for the Republican nomination; and when Washington read the first draft of Taft's acceptance speech, he was dismayed to find a statement supporting black disfranchisement laws in the South. Washington removed the statement and inserted a new one in which Taft would endorse fully the Thirteenth, Fourteenth, and Fifteenth Amendments to the Constitution. Taft accepted the change.

W.E.B. Du Bois supported the Democratic

candidate, William Jennings Bryan, in the election, even though Bryan was vocal in his support for black disfranchisement and lynchings. For blacks, the election of 1908 appeared to be the lesser of two evils, and that was Taft.

After Taft was elected, he asked Washington to advise him on racial matters. Washington accepted, but insisted as always that it not be an official appointment. Taft allowed his adviser to cut out most of the statements in his inaugural address that would be offensive to blacks. However, he refused to delete a statement that he would not appoint blacks to offices in the South where it might cause racial tension. It was extremely disappointing to Washington when Taft lived up to his promise, not only ceasing to appoint blacks in the South but gradually removing those who already held offices.

But the greatest shock of 1908 was a race riot that occurred in Springfield, Illinois, the hometown of Abraham Lincoln. Six blacks were killed by a white mob, and an estimated two-thousand more driven from town. Encouraged by presidents and presidential candidates, northern whites had acquired a lynching mood.

Some northern white liberals perceived that

the division of African-American leadership between Washington and Du Bois was contributing to this. In the hope of unifying blacks, one such man, Oswald Garrison Villard, proposed a conference of blacks and white liberals to form an organization in which all could work together for equal justice. In his invitation to Washington to attend, Villard clearly pointed out that this was not to be an organization controlled by the interests of either Washington or Du Bois but one that would represent all views.

Washington politely declined the invitation, claiming other plans. Some have contended that Washington boycotted the meeting, but this does not appear to be true. In his letter to Villard, Washington stated that his presence at the meeting might "inhibit discussion and might even move the organization in directions it did not want to go." He also emphasized that "there is a work to be done which no one placed in my position can do, which no one living in the South perhaps can do. There is a work which those of us who live here in the South can do, which persons who do not live in the South cannot do."

He was clearly stating that he recognized the importance of other approaches to resolving racial injustice, but that the role he had chosen as "compromiser" was also important, and he could not now give that up.

The organization formed at this conference in New York was first called the National Negro Committee, but it later joined with the Niagara Movement and became the NAACP, the National Association for the Advancement of Colored People. Contrary to the popular view, Washington did not oppose its formation; rather, it was Du Bois and his supporters who fought at the initial meeting to exclude Washington and anyone else who might be friendly to him. Du Bois was to attain leadership in the new organization and would eventually be given the credit for its formation, though it was in fact Oswald Garrison Villard who conceived it and brought the founding membership together.

The founding of the NAACP effectively ended Booker T. Washington's position of spokesman for the majority of African-Americans. Many of his friends, especially those in the North, would abandon him. Yet in most quarters he continued to be revered as a great educator and as a man who had advanced the cause of African-Americans at a critical time in history.

Chapter Nine

Betrayed by Violence

IT IS IMPOSSIBLE TO know what might have happened if Washington had joined forces with Du Bois in the formation of the NAACP. There is a common belief that there is strength in unity, but the approaches of the two men were so polarized there was no common ground. However, Washington continually made a distinction between racial problems in the South and those in the North, and they were different, as different as Du Bois and Washington were themselves.

Du Bois was twelve years younger than Washington, born three years after the end of

---

George Washington Carver and Henry Ford, the automobile tycoon. Ford so admired Carver's work that he later moved his birth cabin to the Ford Museum in Dearborn, Michigan.

the Civil War in Massachusetts. Educated at Fisk University and Harvard, his experience in facing racial prejudice was relatively minor until he went to Atlanta University in 1897 to teach. Although he did live in the South until 1910, he had no emotional tie to it, as did southern whites and blacks.

Washington actually liked southern whites; he considered them as being basically good at heart. However, they resented being forced to do things the way they had been during the Reconstruction period, and as a result, they would now resort to extreme measures at the slightest threat of a return to those ways. What Washington was striving for was to convince southern whites that southern blacks no longer posed such a threat. Once they accepted this, he believed the whites would generously "give" the blacks their rights.

The fact is that the majority of southern whites never ceased feeling threatened by blacks, to some extent because of the demands of black militants like Du Bois and Trotter, but mostly because of the opportunism of politicians such as Roosevelt, Taft, and several generations of state and local office-holders.

Washington held fast to his belief, even with the gradual disaffection of friends, both black and white. He had grown accustomed to emotional isolation, even to paranoia, and his stoicism increased. However, during this time when other friends were deserting him, Washington developed an unlikely friendship with George Washington Carver. For years Carver had been the cause for many irritating problems at Tuskegee, which Washington had tolerated because Carver's work brought success and prestige to his agricultural department.

Now Washington began to call upon Carver in the middle of the night, and the two men would take long walks about the sleeping campus, talking, sharing their thoughts and dreams and problems. These walks apparently helped to sustain Washington for a time.

Washington continued to serve as adviser to the President, though Taft rarely heeded the advice. Washington continually argued for reappointment of black officials, and finally Taft did make a significant concession, appointing William H. Lewis assistant attorney general, the highest ranking black official until the New Deal.

In the late summer and early fall of 1910, Washington sought to rest with a trip to Europe. This time, however, he did not intend to spend all his time relaxing, but decided he wanted to study the conditions of the peasants and the poor in European countries as a comparison with blacks in the United States, so he toured with his principal ghost-writer, Robert E. Park. In the last few years, several books had been published under Washington's name, including *Working with the Hands* (1904), *Tuskegee and Its People* (1905), *Frederick Douglass* (1907), and *The Story of a Negro* (1909).

Again Washington was deluged with invitations to speak and to dine with important people, including the King and Queen of Denmark. He did accept some invitations but turned down many simply because of lack of time. After the problems he faced in his own country, it probably felt good to him to be received so warmly abroad. Wherever he went, he saw conditions of poverty much worse than in the United States. He was convinced that, whatever the discrimination against African-Americans, they were still better off economically than even the most progressive countries of Europe.

He made the mistake of saying this in some of his speeches. One in particular, before the Anti-Slavery and Aborigines Protection Society in London, was inaccurately reported back to the National Negro Committee in the United States, and Du Bois hotly sent off an open letter to Europe stating that Washington was not a recognized spokesman for African-Americans and that "the Negro problem in America" is not "in process of satisfactory solution."

This was not what Washington had said, but the difference highlighted the essential differences between Du Bois, who was concerned about civil rights, and Washington, whose main interest was the economic well-being of blacks. The book that resulted from this trip was *The Man Farthest Down*, published in 1912.

Washington returned home in October by way of New York and Boston, where he was received with enthusiasm.

He went on the offensive, attacking the National Negro Committee, Du Bois, and Villard for the letter sent to Europe attacking him. From this point on, there would be no reconciling the two sides.

Increasingly Washington was suffering health problems, primarily digestive in nature, though he also had severe headaches. On a visit to Boston in 1910, he was temporarily immobilized, confined to his room at the Parker House with an attack of indigestion, one of the few times his health condition was mentioned in the press.

Early in 1911, he visited the Battle Creek Sanitarium in Michigan, run by Dr. J.H. Kellogg, an early proponent of a health-food diet, emphasizing the importance of vegetables to digestion. Washington improved rapidly and was greatly impressed by Kellogg.

From Battle Creek, Washington traveled to New York, arriving there on March 18 and checking into the Hotel Manhattan. The next day, a Sunday, he gave speeches at two churches, one white and one black, then returned to the hotel. This was one of the rare occasions that Washington traveled alone, unaccompanied by his traveling secretary. While he had been in Battle Creek, his secretary at Tuskegee, Emmett Scott, had written to him to suggest that he get together with the Tuskegee auditor, Daniel Cranford Smith, who would be visiting some friends in New York when Washington was there. Since he had nothing else to do for the evening, he decided to try seeing Smith.

Washington no longer had the letter, and he tried to remember the address and the name of the people Smith was to be visiting. He recalled the name as "McCrary" or "McClure" and the address as being on Sixty-third Street.

It turned out to be a slightly less than respectable area of the city, consisting mostly of theatrical boarding houses, though some of the women on the street appeared to be prostitutes. He approached the house thought to have been the one in Scott's letter and scanned the names on the directory. Finding a name that seemed close, he rang the bell. But there was no answer.

While he was in the vestibule, an attractive white woman in her thirties passed through with her dog from inside the building. Getting no response to his ring, Washington left the building and began to walk up and down the street, trying to decide whether he should approach another house or if perhaps he had the street wrong. Finally believing this was the correct address, he returned to the vestibule and rang the bell again.

Again he got no answer, and again he returned to the street to walk about for awhile. When he went into the vestibule for the third time, a heavy-set white man charged in after him drunkenly demanding to know what he was doing there, and before Washington could reply the man started beating him.

Attempting to protect himself from the man's blows, Washington ran into the street, followed by his assailant, who grabbed a cane from another man and used it to pummel Washington further. Washington fled toward

Central Park, which was only a short distance away. As he approached the park, Washington fell, but there was a policeman nearby who intervened.

The assailant claimed that Washington was a thief he had caught attempting to break into his apartment and demanded that he be arrested.

As a crowd gathered, the policeman, a plainclothesman named Chester A. Hagan, arrested Washington, who was now bleeding profusely from wounds to his head, and turned him over to a uniformed policeman to be taken to the stationhouse.

The burly attacker pressed charges against Washington, giving his name as Henry Albert Ulrich. Washington had two large wounds on his head, as well as one on his ear, but these were ignored while he was booked on a charge of attempted burglary.

When Washington gave his name, at first the lieutenant who was booking him refused to believe it. Washington provided proof, the charges were dropped immediately, and the lieutenant called for an ambulance. He then asked Washington if he wished to press charges against his assailant, which Washington did, for felonious assault. Ulrich was promptly arrested, charged, and placed under bail.

The woman who came in to pay Ulrich's bail, claiming to be his wife, was the one who had first passed through the vestibule with her dog when Washington was scanning the directory. She was highly offended that her husband had been arrested and the black man had been released. She claimed that Washington had attempted to molest her, approaching her and addressing her, "Hello, sweetheart."

The story of the attack hit the newspapers the next morning, with a picture of the bandaged Washington, but giving only the Ulrichs' version of what happened before Washington had the opportunity to tell his side of the story. What registered in people's minds first was what held: this was confirmation of the stereotype that even the most upstanding black man could not resist molesting white women.

When Washington finally managed to tell his story, it seemed feeble and unlikely. Even though Ulrich was the one who was legally on trial, it was the black leader who was being tried by the press, the one who was asked to prove that he was telling the truth. Washington could not produce the letter from Scott that he claimed had directed him to Sixty-third Street, and it would be several days before Scott and Smith would arrive to try to corroborate his story, but even then Smith denied having any association with that seedy neighborhood on the edge of the Tenderloin district, and he certainly had not given that address for Washington to meet him.

At the court hearing, Ulrich claimed he had not struck Washington at all, that Washington was drunk and his injuries had been caused by his falling on the street. He went even further by claiming that Washington had cursed at him and had actually attempted to strike him. Most people were aware, however, that Washington did not drink, and that in fact he was a staunch prohibitionist.

For weeks the press carried front-page stories on the incident, pointing out all the sordid possibilities for Washington being in such a questionable white neighborhood. Many public figures came to Washington's defense—Andrew Carnegie, President Taft, former President Roosevelt—and there were demonstrations of support from church groups. However, the white supremacist views predominated, and a fund was set up for Ulrich's legal defense.

The legal maneuverings lasted for six months, and so did the press coverage and the public debate over Washington's "guilt" in the matter, much of it based on information stemming from rumors or conjecture, as well as upon the assumption—by both blacks and whites—that a black man had no right to be in a white neighborhood without a specific purpose.

It was revealed that the supposed "Mrs. Ulrich" wasn't really married to the defendant but was actually only living with him, that she was in fact named Laura Page Alvarez, a woman of dubious morals and reputation, estranged from Mr. Alvarez. The real Mrs. Ulrich lived in New Jersey and had been unable to locate her husband until reading about the case in the newspapers; she was suing him for desertion and failure to support their children.

Even these facts failed to help Washington. If anything they seemed to substantiate the public's suspicion that Washington had been drunk and had gone into the neighborhood seeking out a white prostitute. The myth that had been built up in recent years, that a black man who had been drinking had only one thing on his mind, sex with a white woman, had become totally ingrained in white consciousness.

Even the newly formed NAACP did more harm than good when its public statement did not defend Washington personally but merely expressed "regrets" at the assault and pointed out that it gave "renewed evidence of racial discrimination."

To make matters worse, none of the witnesses to the incident, the people on the street or looking from their houses, came forward to testify in court. Two years later, one woman wrote to Washington personally to say that she had witnessed what happened and confirmed that his version was the true one.

Overwhelmed by the adverse publicity, Washington accepted the advice of lawyers and attempted to settle the matter out of court. Their concern was that the New York courts were so graft-ridden that Washington had a chance of losing, despite the evidence. However, the public took this as an admission of guilt on his part, so he continued to wait for the trial.

The case came before a panel of three judges in November of 1911. The decision was two to one in favor of Ulrich. Already having been found guilty by the press and public opinion, Washington was now found guilty by the courts, even though he had not been the man on trial.

Maggie Washington, the third wife of Booker T. Washington. An extremely strong woman, she threw herself into helping him in his work—and making sure that he did not overwork himself.

Chapter Ten

Past His Time

WASHINGTON RETURNED TO HIS work undaunted by the sordid Ulrich affair, facing the future with his usual stoicism. His formerly spotless image was now tarnished, but he continued to draw enthusiastic crowds wherever he spoke, and the amount of money he raised for Tuskegee was not lessened. His books, *My Larger Education,* published in 1911, and *The Man Farthest Down,* in 1912, sold well. However, several members of the Tuskegee Board of Trustees resigned because of the Ulrich affair, and whispers and rumors continued to follow him.

Erected in honor of Booker T. Washington, the statue "Lifting the Veil of Ignorance," signifies Washington's life-long dedication to bringing the African-American to greater hights.

Despite it all, no one could deny what he had achieved at Tuskegee.

President Taft continued to call upon Washington for advice, and there is no indication that he listened to his adviser any less than he had before. However, Taft had done so little to support black interests it was difficult to judge whether the President had lost confidence in Washington. In the last two years of the Taft administration, there were a few black appointments, but primarily to positions in the diplomatic services in African countries.

In the 1912 election year, Washington found himself in a quandry. Former President Roosevelt decided to oppose Taft for the Republican nomination, and when he did not succeed he formed the Progressive Party to run against Taft and Democratic Party nominee, Woodrow Wilson, in the election. Washington chose not to support either Roosevelt or Taft openly.

It is generally believed that this was due to his unwillingness to make a public choice between the two candidates, both of them his friends. However, this would not have prevented Washington from attempting to have the Republican platform include a positive statement for blacks. It seems more likely that he was sensitive about the possibility that, because of the Ulrich affair, his support might have a negative effect on either or both of the candidates.

Privately, Washington expressed a preference for Taft, and it is likely that he voted for him. Washington's enemies, Du Bois and Trotter, supported the Democratic candidate, Woodrow Wilson, despite Wilson's and the Democratic Party's poor record on racial matters.

Wilson won the election, and upon taking office immediately began removing blacks from government positions, an action that the NAACP did not object to because most of the black appointments had been made on the recommendation of Booker T. Washington. Not only was the new president a southerner by birth, but at this time southern senators and representatives rose to powerful positions in Congress, resulting in an increase in segregationist legislation, the most serious of which was a bill to bar foreign-born blacks from immigrating to the United States.

Washington joined with other black leaders around the country in actively fighting this bill, ultimately succeeding in defeating it in the House after it had passed the Senate.

During this period Washington appeared to

age rapidly; at times he seemed to be weak, even feeble. He was only in his mid-fifties, but he looked much older. The stress of the Ulrich affair on top of years of overwork was taking its toll. His energy may also have been affected by the realization that times were changing, and that for African-Americans the changes were for the worse, especially in the South.

He must have wondered if his approach of accommodationism might not have been wrong after all, for when he had started southern blacks at least had the right to vote. Now, even though they had acquired a degree of economic power, they were losing political power.

Beginning in 1912, Washington renewed his efforts to end discrimination on the railroads. He wrote letters to the managers of railway companies and articles for magazines accepting the separation of facilities but protesting the inequality. Not only were blacks relegated to baggage cars (or to boxcars behind the baggage cars) but they were provided with only one restroom for both sexes, and the facilities, including waiting rooms in depots, were poorly maintained and invariably filthy.

During 1913, his children would prove to a source of pride to him, having matured and put most of their serious problems behind them. On New Year's Eve, Booker Jr. married Nettie Hancock in Houston, Texas, and Washington built the couple a house in Greenwood Village, also financing construction of a business building for his son. Dave married Edith Merriwether in Atlantic City, New Jersey. Portia moved to Dallas, Texas, where she obtained a job teaching music in a high school. And young Laura enrolled in Spelman Seminary in Atlanta.

At this time, Washington had an increasing interest in health, diet, and preventive medicine, possibly because of his own worsening physical condition. The John A. Andrew Hospital at Tuskegee was constructed and dedicated, and in 1914, when Washington organized the Tuskegee Negro Conference, one day of the activities centered on public health and on improving diet and hygiene among blacks.

This concern for health would come too late for Booker T. Washington. In 1914 and 1915, his physical condition deteriorated rapidly, yet he did not slow down his hectic travel and speaking schedule. In the spring of 1915 he continued his annual speaking tours of southern states, this time focusing on Louisiana. He was there when D.W. Griffith's

With Tuskegee Institute campus finally completed, Booker T. Washington realized the dream he'd cherished for so many years, to offer a quality education to African-Americans in the

deep south, had finally come to pass. But there was still the never-ending problem of funds to keep the college going as most of the student could not afford to pay for their education.

movie, *Birth of a Nation,* opened, based on the racist novel of Thomas Dixon, Jr., *The Clansman.*

Du Bois and the NAACP were vocal in opposition to the film, recommending a boycott. Washington was asked for a response, and his suggestion was that it simply be ignored; to protest it would serve only to give it publicity.

Also that spring, Washington was informed that his sister Amanda Johnston had suffered a stroke. He interrupted his speaking schedule to go to Malden to spend time with her before she died.

In August, he went to Boston to give his annual address to the National Negro Business League. He was seriously ill at the time, but he managed to get through the speech.

At the end of the summer he did take a break for a brief vacation, going with several other Tuskegee administrators on a fishing trip to Coden near Mobile Bay, on the Alabama coast. He had been vacationing there annually since 1913.

When Washington left Coden, he was still not feeling well, and he wrote to the Mayo brothers clinic in Rochester, Minnesota, inquiring about the possibility of going there. He received a welcoming response, but he had yet to find a time in his busy schedule to squeeze in medical attention. He had become obsessive about his public responsibilities to the detriment of personal concerns such as his sister's funeral and his own health.

On October 17, he gave a Sunday evening talk to the students at Tuskegee on the subject of "Team Work," and then left for New Haven, Connecticut, where he was scheduled to give two speeches on October 25. One of these was for the A.M.E. Zion Church in New Haven, and the other was for the American Missionary Association and the National Council of Congregational Churches, held in Woolsey Hall at Yale. After the Yale speech, Washington spoke briefly with former President Taft who was one of the honored guests for the occasion. He was already suffering one of his "attacks" of abdominal pain.

After finishing his speech at Zion Church, Washington did not spend the night in New Haven but took the boat for New York, where he was scheduled to speak the next day.

He had a rugged schedule ahead of him, first to return to Tuskegee, then to Fisk University, and on to Petersburg, Virginia, by November 5 for a speech before the Negro Organization Society of Virginia, which he had tried unsuccessfully to cancel for an engagement in North Dakota. Despite his condition,

Washington managed to keep several meetings he had scheduled in New York, including one with two of Tuskegee's trustees who were concerned about his health.

One of them, William G. Willcox, literally forced Washington to see a doctor, a friend of his, Dr. Walter A. Bastedo, who was a specialist in abdominal diseases. Dr. Bastedo insisted that Washington check into St. Luke's Hospital for tests. Reluctantly, Washington canceled his scheduled trips and took the doctor's advice, checking into the hospital on November 5. Upon receiving word of her husband's decision, Maggie Washington set out by train for New York.

Dr. Bastedo quickly determined that Washington was suffering from a serious kidney problem; he also had extremely high blood pressure, hardening of the arteries, and was suffering from stress and nervous exhaustion. He forced his patient to remain in the hospital for further tests, and he called in other doctors to consult.

Word of Washington's hospitalization reached the press on November 10, when the New York *Tribune* revealed that he was "suffering from a nervous breakdown." Reporters flocked to St. Luke's Hospital, and despite Washington's objections, Dr. Bastedo issued a statement to them about his patient's condition. To make matters worse, in listing off Washington's medical problems, the doctor made a reference to "racial characteristics," which some interpreted to mean that he was suffering from syphillis.

On the afternoon of November 12, over the objections of the doctors, who insisted that Washington might have only hours or days to live and certainly could not survive a journey, Maggie checked her husband out of St. Luke's, and they boarded a train for Tuskegee. This was Washington's wish, not only because of the indiscretion of Dr. Bastedo in breaking doctor-patient confidentiality but because, if he was going to die, he wanted to do it at his beloved Tuskegee. His statement issued to the press was: "I was born in the South, I have lived and labored in the South, and I expect to die and be buried in the South."

When their train arrived at Chehaw, the junction for Tuskegee, the following evening, it was met by Washington's secretary Emmett Scott, his son Booker Jr., his brother John Henry, and an ambulance. He was not taken to the Tuskegee hospital but to his bed at home.

There in his sleep, he died the next morning at 4:45. The date was November 14, 1915;

he was fifty-nine years old.

He had told Maggie that he did not want an elaborate funeral, with eulogies, pomp, and ceremony, and he wished to be buried in the cemetery beside the Tuskegee chapel with a plain headstone. However, so many people, black and white, arrived at Tuskegee to pay their last respects, she decided to allow the body to lie in state in the chapel for a day before the funeral.

The line of mourners that passed by the open casket on November 16 seemed endless, and their grief was genuine. Whatever kind of man Washington had been, he had been like no other who had come before or would come after, and he had touched each one of them, reaching a special place in their souls.

Booker Taliaferro Washington had risen from obscurity and faced all obstacles with courage and determination to change the world around him for the better. He left behind him a legacy of hope and faith that people could work together regardless of race, creed, or color.

And there was one thing that even his enemies could agree upon: he had always done what he believed was right.

INDEX

A.M.E. Zion Church, New Haven, Connecticut, 183
Adams, Lewis, 81, 85
Africa, 131, 155, 156
African-Americans 48, 58, 69, 74–76, 79–80, 90, 93, 101, 104, 110–111, 114, 118, 120, 124, 132, 142–145, 155–156, 158–159, 164–165, 178
Afro-American League, Louisville, 138
Alabama, 79, 108
Alabama Hall, 105
Alabama Legislature, 80
Alabama State Teachers Association, 110
Albany, Ohio, Enterprise Academy, 87
Alvarez, Laura Page "Mrs. Henry A. Ulrich", 171
American Indians, 75
American Missionary Association, 60, 183
Anthony, Susan B., 131, 132
Appomattox Courthouse, 36
Arkansas, 145
Armstrong, General Samuel Chapman, 61–62, 73, 75, 78–80
Athens, Ohio, 106
Atkinson, George W., 132
Atlanta Compromise, the, 118, 132, 183
Atlanta Exposition in 1895, 12, 113
Atlanta Riot, 150
Atlanta University, 162
Atlanta, Georgia, 114, 115, 150–152
Bailey, Alonzo, 154
Baker, Williams, 107

Bastedo, Dr. Walter A., 184, 185
Battle Creek Sanitarium, Michigan, 166
Bedford, Reverend Robert C., 96
Berlin, Germany, 153
Birth of a Nation, film, 182
"Black Belt", 84
"black cabinet, the", 124
"blueback speller", 41
Boston, Massachusetts, 128, 165, 182
Boston Riot, 142
Bowen plantation, 87, 89
Bowen, William Banks, 81
Bradford Academy, 136
Brown, John, 19
"Brownsville Riots, the", 150, 156
Brownsville, Texas, 149, 151
Bryan, William Jennings, 157
Buffalo, New York, 145
"Bull Run" (*also see* Battle of Manassas), 30
Bullock, Rufus, 116
Burroughs family, 25, 31, 32, 37
Burroughs plantation, 24, 27–28, 36–37, 40
Burroughs, Elizabeth, 20–21, 28, 30, 36–37
Burroughs, Ellen, 25, 28, 40
Burroughs, James, 20–22, 28, 30
Burroughs, Laura, 25, 28, 40
Butler's Chapel A.M.E. Zion Church, 81
Campbell, George W., 81
Cardwell, John W., 86
Carnegie Hall, 141
Carnegie, Andrew, 134, 138, 148, 170

187

Carver, George Washington, 121, 148, 163
Central Park, 168
Character Building, book, Booker T. Washington, 134
Charleston, West Virginia, 71
Chehaw, Alabama, 185
Chicago Peace Jubilee, 1898, 11, 124
Chicago, Illinois, 124, 156
Cincinnati, Selma, and Mobile Railroad, 104
City Council of Chaleston, West Virginia, 132
Civil War, 28, 60, 81, 101, 111, 121, 142, 162
Clansman, The, book, Thomas Dixon, Jr., 182
Cleveland, President Grover, 120, 138
Coden, Alabama, 182
Columbian Exposition, Chicago, Illinois, 1893, 113
Columbus Avenue A.M.E. Church, 139
Confederate Army, 30
Conference for Education in the South, 153
Congregational Church, Montgomery, Alabama, 96
Congress, 152, 155, 177
Connecticut, 68
Dallas, Texas, 179
Davidson, James C., 87
Davidson, Joseph, 87
Davidson, Olivia A., (*also see* Olivia A. Davidson Washington), 86–88, 90, 106
Davis, William, 41–42, 46
Democratic Party, 176
Denmark, King and Queen of, 164
disfranchisement, 125, 144, 156–157
Douglass, Frederick, 111

Du Bois, W.E.B., 128, 139, 141–143, 145, 148–149, 151, 156, 158–159, 161–162, 164–165, 177
Dummer Academy, Massachusetts, 136
Dunbar, Paul Lawrence, 128
Dyer, Thomas B., 81
Eastman, George, 134
El Caney, Cuba, 125
Elliott, Dr. Noah, 106
Elliott, Mary, 106
Emancipation, 36
Emancipation Proclamation, 37
England, 131, 155
Europe, 142, 163, 165
Ferguson, Amanda, (*also see* Amanda Ferguson Johnston), 27, 31, 38, 64
Ferguson, Jane, 20–22, 30–31, 37–38, 40–42, 49, 64
Ferguson, Josiah 22, 27, 31
Ferguson, Wash, 27, 31–32, 38, 40–42, 46, 64
Fifteenth Amendment to the Constitution, 156
Fifty-fourth Massachusetts Regiment, 120
Fisk University, Nashville, Tennessee, 153, 162, 183
"Force that Wins, The", speech, 73
Fort Brown, Texas, 149
Fourteenth Amendment to the Constitution, 156
Framingham State Normal School in Massachusetts, 87, 122
France, 131, 155
Franklin County, Virginia, 20
Frederick Douglass, book (1907), 164
Freedmen's Bureau school, 87
Friesland, oceanliner, 130
Fuller, Supreme Court Justice Melville Weston, 131

Georgia, 32, 117
Germany, 155
Graduation ceremonies, June, 1875, 66
Greenwood Village, 179
Griffith, D.W., 179
Guardian, the, 138, 143
Hagan Chester A., 168
Hague, The, 131
Hale's Ford, 20, 22, 55
Hampton Normal and Agricultural Institute, 48-49, 52-53, 56-58, 60-62, 64-66, 68, 70-73, 75-76, 78, 80, 84, 87-88, 90, 108, 114, 122
Hampton Alumni Association, 100
Hancock, Nettie, 179
Harlan, Supreme Court Justice John Marshall, 131
Harrison, President Benjamin, 131
Harvard University, 120, 162
Hayes, Mrs. Rutherford B., 87
Hollis Street Theater, 128
Hopkins, Charles T., 152
Hotel Manhattan, 166
House of Commons, 131
House of Representatives, 177
Hunter, General David, 32
International Meeting of Christian Workers, 114
Iowa State, 121
Jameson, Eleanor, 107
"Jim Crow", 105
John A. Andrew Hospital, Tuskegee, Alabama, 179
Johnston, Albert, 137
Johnston, Amanda Ferguson, (*also see* Amanda Ferguson) 137, 182
Johnston, Clara, 137
Kaiser Wilhelm II, oceanliner, 139
Kanawha County, West Virginia, 32

Kanawha Salines (salt furnaces), 32
Kansas, 19
Kellogg, Dr. J.H., 166
Ku Klux Klan, 69-70, 87, 101
Law and Order Clubs, 153
Lee, Robert E., 36
Lewis, William H., 163
Liberia, 155
Lincoln, Abraham, 157
Lincoln University, 110
Logan, Warren, 110, 121
Louisiana Purchase Celebration, St. Louis, Missouri, 1904, 113
Lynchburg, Virginia, 32
Mackie, Mary Fletcher, 58-60, 62, 65, 88
Macon County, Alabama, 80, 84, 104, 105
Macon, Mississippi, 109
Madison Square Garden, 138
Madison, Wisconsin, 100
Malden, West Virginia, 38, 41, 43, 48, 53, 55, 63-64, 68-71, 75, 80, 90-91, 182
Man Farthest Down, The, book (1912), 165, 175
Manassas, Battle of (*also see* "Bull Run"), 30
Mark Twain, 131
Marshall, James Fowle Baldwin, 63, 84, 86, 88, 99-100
Massachusetts, 108, 111, 162
Mayo Brothers Clinic, 182
McKinley, President William, 10-12, 124-125, 128, 144
Memphis, Tennessee, 87
Merchant of Venice, The, 99
Merriwether, Edith, 179
Mississippi, 87
Mobile Bay, Alabama, 182
Monroe, (slave) Jane's half-brother, 21

Montgomery *Advertiser,* 104
Montgomery, Alabama, 104
Morgan, Clement, 143
Morgan, S. Griffits, 61
Murray, James, 109
Murray, Laura, 137, 179
Murray, Lucy, 109
Murray, Thomas J., 137
My Larger Education, book (1911), 175
National Association for the Advancement of Colored People (NAACP), 159, 161, 171, 177, 182
National Council of Congregational Churches, 183
National Education Association, 100–101
National Negro Business League, Boston, 138, 182
National Negro Committee, 159, 164–165
"Negro Building," 114, 120
Negro Organization Society of Virginia, 183
New Deal, 163
New Haven, Connecticut, 183
New Orleans Exposition, 1885, 113
New York *Evening Post,* 106
New York *World,* 116
New York City, New York, 130, 150, 165
New York *Tribune,* 184
Niagara Falls, 145
Niagara Movement, 145, 159
North Carolina, 22
North Dakota, 183
Oberlin College, 136
Ogden, Robert C., 134
Ohio, 41
Oklahoma, 145
Old Point Comfort, 63
Opelika, Alabama, 105
Oval Room, 10

Pan-American Exposition, Buffalo, New York, 1901, 113
Park, Robert E., 164
Parker House, 165
Peace Jubilee in Atlanta, 125
Petersburg, Virginia, 183
Phillips Exeter Academy, 153
Phoebus, Harrison, 62
Pierce, Moses, 90
Pinkerton agents, 149
Pitman, William Sidney, 153
Porter Hall, 89, 94–96, 98
Porter, Alfred Haynes, 89
Pottawatomie Creek, Kansas, 20
Princeton, 120
Progressive Party, 176
Prohibition, 154
Queen Victoria, 131–132
Reconstruction period, 74, 143, 162
Republican Party, 124, 144–145, 156
Rice, Lewis, minister, 41
Richmond, Virginia, 56
riot, Lawrence, Kansas, 20
Rockefeller Hall, 134
Rockefeller, John D., Jr., 134
Roosevelt, Archie, 11
Roosevelt, Ethel, 11
Roosevelt, Mrs. Theodore (nee Edith Kermit Carow), 10–12
Roosevelt, President Theodore 10–12, 16, 132, 144–145, 150–153, 156, 162, 170, 176
Roosevelt, Quentin, 11
Rough Riders, 10
Ruffner, General Lewis 49, 70
Ruffner, Mrs. Lewis (Viola), 49–50, 59, 64
Saint-Gaudens, Augustus, 120
salt furnace, 46, 49, 52
San Juan Hill, 10, 144
Santiago, Cuba, 125

Scott, Emmett, 144, 148, 166, 169, 185
Senate, 177
Shaw, Robert Gould, Memorial, 120
Slater, John Fox, 90
Smith, Celia, Fanny's mother, 68, 91
Smith, Daniel Cranford, Tuskegee auditor, 166, 170
Smith, Fanny Norton, (*also see* Fanny Norton Smith Washington), 68, 79, 90–91
Smith, Samuel, 68, 91, 94
Snodgrass, Margaret E., 86
Sophia, (slave) Jane's half-sister, 21
Souls of Black Folk, The, book, W.E.B. DuBois, 142
Southampton, England, 132
Sowing and Reaping, book, Booker T. Washington, 134
Spanish-American War, 10, 124
Spelman Seminary, Atlanta, Georgia, 179
Springfield, Illinois race riot of 1908, 157
St. Louis, oceanliner, 132
St. Luke's Hospital, 184, 185
Stanley, Sir Henry M., 131
Stokes, Olivia E. Phelps Scholarship, 155
Story of My Life and Work, The, book, Booker T. Washington, 134
Story of a Negro, The, book (1909), 164
Suppression of the Slave Trade, The, book, by W.E.B. DuBois, 128
Supreme Court, 155
Swanson, M.B., 81
Taft, President William Howard, 157, 162–163, 170, 176–177, 183
Taft, William Howard, Secretary of War, 150, 152, 156
Taliaferro family, 22
Taliaferro, Harden, Baptist preacher, 22
Tanner, Henry O., 131
Taylor, Reverend I.C., 91
"Team Work," speech, 183
Tenderloin District, 170
Tennessee Pullman Segregation Law, 141
Thirteenth Amendment to the Constitution, 156
Thompson, Waddy, 89
Tiffany glass screens, 10
tobacco crops, 20
Togo, 156
Trotter, Monroe, 138–139, 141–143, 148, 162, 177
Tuskegee, Alabama, 16, 80–81, 84–85, 91, 98–100, 183, 185
Tuskegee and Its People, book (1905), 164
Tuskegee Board of Trustees, 175, 184
Tuskegee Chapel, 186
Tuskegee Institute, 12, 80, 86–88, 90, 93–95, 99, 104–111, 114, 118, 121, 125, 128, 130, 134, 136–138, 143, 148, 155, 163, 166, 175–176, 182
Tuskegee Institute Cemetery, 100
Tuskegee Institute Savings Bank, 137
Tuskegee Institute teachers, 104, 105
Tuskegee merchants, 98
Tuskegee Negro Conference, 179
Tuskegee Normal School, 80
Tuskegee Training School, 136
Ulrich, Henry Albert, 168–170, 172, 175, 177–178
Ulrich, Mrs. Henry Albert, 171

"Uncle Tom," 154
Union Army, 30
Unitarian Club of Boston, 110
United States, 11, 17, 19, 111, 149, 153, 164, 177
United States Congress, 114
United States annexation of Cuba, speech, 66
University Club, 131
Up from Slavery, autobiography, Booker T. Washington, 22, 69, 134
Vermont, 49
Villard, Oswald Garrison, 158–159, 165
Virginia, 22, 25, 32, 36, 48, 55–56, 60
Washington, Baker Taliaferro (*also see* Booker T, Washington, Jr.), 107, 122
Washington, Booker T., 10–11, 20–21, 24–28, 31–33, 36–38, 40–43, 46–50, 52–53, 55–66, 68, 70–71, 73–74, 76, 78–81, 84–91, 93–95, 98–101, 104, 106, 108, 110–111, 113, 115–116, 118, 120–122, 124–125, 128, 130–132, 134, 137–139, 141, 143–144, 150–165, 168–170, 172, 175, 177–179, 184–186
Washington, Booker T. Jr. (*also see* Baker Taliaferro Washington), 107, 136, 153, 179, 185
Washington, Booker T., Industrial Institute of Liberia, 155
Washington, D.C., 9, 12, 71, 125
Washington, Ernest Davidson (Dave), 107, 122, 136–137, 153, 179
Washington, Fanny Norton (*also see* Fanny Norton Smith), 93–94, 96, 98–100
Washington, James, 43, 64, 70, 79
Washington, John Henry, 21, 26–27, 30, 38, 43, 53, 64, 70, 121, 185
Washington, Margaret James Murray (Maggie), 109, 115, 122, 124, 128, 130–132, 184–186
Washington, Olivia A. Davidson, (*also see* Olivia A. Davidson), 107–109
Washington, Portia Marshall, 99, 107, 109–110, 122, 134, 153, 179
Wayland Seminary, 70–71
Wellesley College, 136
Wellesley School for Boys, 136
West Virginia, 38, 62
Wheeling, West Virginia, 62
White House, the, 9–11, 16, 132, 151
Whiting, Robert, 9
"Wigwam, The", 76
Willcox, William G., 184
Wilmington, Delaware, 125
Wilson, President Woodrow, 176
Windsor Castle, 131
Woolsey Hall, Yale, 183
Working with the Hands, book (1904), 164

PICTURE CREDITS

Christopher de Gasperi: pp. 8, 13–15, 23, 34, 67, 82–83, 119, 129, 133, 135, 140, 180–181; The Schomburg Center for Research in Black Culture, New York Public Library: pp. 54, 146–147, 174; Library of Congress: pp. 29, 39, 44–45, 51, 72, 112, 126–127, 160; Hampton Institute: p. 77; Tuskegee Instituie: pp. 92, 97, 123, 173.